# Inspirations From Kent
Edited by Annabel Cook

 Young**Writers**

First published in Great Britain in 2007 by:
Young Writers
Remus House
Coltsfoot Drive
Peterborough
PE2 9JX
Telephone: 01733 890066
Website: www.youngwriters.co.uk

SB ISBN 978-1 84431 118 7

# Foreword

Young Writers was established in 1991 and has been passionately devoted to the promotion of reading and writing in children and young adults ever since. The quest continues today. Young Writers remains as committed to the nurturing of poetic and literary talent as ever.

This year's Young Writers competition has proven as vibrant and dynamic as ever and we are delighted to present a showcase of the best poetry from across the UK and in some cases overseas. Each poem has been selected from a wealth of *Little Laureates* entries before ultimately being published in this, our sixteenth primary school poetry series.

Once again, we have been supremely impressed by the overall quality of the entries we have received. The imagination, energy and creativity which has gone into each young writer's entry made choosing the poems a challenging and often difficult but ultimately hugely rewarding task - the general high standard of the work submitted ensured this opportunity to bring their poetry to a larger appreciative audience.

We sincerely hope you are pleased with this final collection and that you will enjoy *Little Laureates Inspirations From Kent* for many years to come.

# Contents

## Lady Joanna Thornhill Primary School

| | |
|---|---|
| Megan Jones  (10) | 14 |
| Jemima Barnes  (9) | 15 |

## Langton Green CP School

| | |
|---|---|
| Emily Coyne | 15 |
| Rhianna Steer  (11) | 15 |
| James Wakelin | 16 |
| Ryan Searle  (10) | 16 |
| Ella Davey | 16 |
| Bethany Noble | 16 |
| Kate Murphy | 17 |

## Long Mead Community Primary School

| | |
|---|---|
| Abigail Teresa Fitzgerald  (7) | 17 |
| Jessie Anderson  (8) | 17 |
| Damian Hammett  (8) | 18 |
| Crystal Dobson  (7) | 18 |
| Jessica Tapp  (7) | 19 |

## Lympne CE Primary School

| | |
|---|---|
| Thomas Hallett  (10) | 19 |
| Ethan Charles Dunlop Wright  (9) | 19 |
| Harry Gibbons  (10) | 20 |
| Megan King  (8) | 20 |
| William Foster  (10) | 20 |
| Francesca Storti  (8) | 21 |
| Emily King  (10) | 21 |
| Amy Ruffell  (9) | 21 |
| Phoebe Bruford  (10) | 22 |
| Sam Hindess  (10) | 22 |
| Frank Morgan  (9) | 22 |
| Robert Leigh  (8) | 23 |
| James Wood  (11) | 23 |
| Cameron McKay  (10) | 23 |
| Rebecca Phillips  (11) | 24 |
| James Pearcy  (11) | 24 |
| Olivia Boutwood  (8) | 24 |
| Sean Wythe  (8) | 25 |
| Jack Bryant  (9) | 25 |

## Mundella Primary School

## Northumberland Heath Primary School

| | |
|---|---|
| Sophie Paczensky  (10) | 64 |
| Skye Matczak  (9) | 64 |
| Ivanca Gay  (9) | 65 |
| Xena Djima  (9) | 65 |
| Jake Brickwood  (9) | 65 |

## Palm Bay CP School

| | |
|---|---|
| Henry Jack Tucker  (9) | 66 |
| Holly Harvey  (9) | 67 |
| Bradley Welsh  (9) | 68 |
| Jack Brightwell  (9) | 68 |
| Chantelle Richardson  (9) | 69 |
| Jordan Childs  (9) | 69 |
| Frederick Hiscock  (9) | 70 |
| Olivia Brooman  (9) | 70 |
| Bradley Anderson  (8) | 71 |
| Alisha Kinnon  (9) | 71 |
| Oliver Murphy  (9) | 72 |
| Katheryn Lamb  (10) | 72 |
| Amy Staiger  (9) | 73 |
| Kieran Somers  (9) | 73 |
| Chelsea Arnold  (9) | 74 |
| Beatrice Hawkins  (9) | 74 |
| Jessica Dummett  (8) | 75 |
| Elisha Kemp  (9) | 75 |
| Ashley Farbrace  (11) | 76 |
| Sophia Philpott  (10) | 76 |
| Jasmine Rio Hitchens  (10) | 77 |
| Chloe Griggs  (8) | 77 |
| Christopher Jordan  (10) | 78 |
| Charlie Sladden  (9) | 79 |
| Jordan Morris  (10) | 80 |
| Frazer England-Fogarty  (9) | 80 |
| Fahmina Begum  (10) | 81 |
| Daniel Christopher Parker  (10) | 82 |
| Lauren Katherine Grainger  (10) | 82 |
| Sarah North  (10) | 83 |
| Kayleigh Kinnon  (10) | 83 |
| Daniel Cunningham  (10) | 84 |
| Sophie Hadley  (10) | 85 |
| Tarek Boumrah  (10) | 86 |

| | |
|---|---|
| Amba-Jo Cawte  (10) | 87 |
| Rosie Raven  (10) | 88 |
| Phoebe Allen  (10) | 89 |
| Jessie-Jo Epps  (10) | 90 |
| Holly Rebecca Austen  (10) | 91 |
| Aaron Barnett  (9) | 91 |
| James Mulligan  (10) | 92 |
| Thomas Syson-Warwick  (9) | 92 |
| Deanna Basson | 92 |
| George Walton  (9) | 93 |
| Amy Holland  (9) | 93 |
| Jake Vial  (9) | 93 |
| Paul Baker  (9) | 94 |
| Cameron Roan Hardwick  (9) | 94 |
| Kate Warburton  (10) | 94 |
| Darrioush Zahedi  (10) | 95 |
| Oli Rahman  (9) | 95 |
| John Christopher Forster  (10) | 95 |
| Edward Martin  (9) | 96 |
| Megan Liddell  (9) | 96 |
| Emma Saunders  (10) | 97 |
| Katie Baldock  (9) | 97 |
| Rory Middleton  (10) | 98 |
| Pablo Garcia Thomas  (9) | 98 |
| Grace Ellisdon  (10) | 99 |
| Charlotte Tonkiss  (9) | 99 |

## St Eanswythe's CE (A) Primary School, Folkestone

| | |
|---|---|
| James Hannah  (11) | 100 |
| Brittany Cousins  (7) | 100 |
| Aimée Thomson  (8) | 101 |
| Trevyn Rayner-Canham  (9) | 101 |
| Jordan Neagle  (11) | 102 |
| Paige Baigent  (11) | 102 |
| Kimberly Stephens  (8) | 103 |
| Charlotte Edgar  (9) | 103 |
| Francesca Marsh  (9) | 104 |
| Tula Williamson  (8) | 104 |
| Hayley Brickell  (11) | 105 |
| Sophie Thomson  (10) | 105 |
| Bethany Read  (10) | 106 |

Connor Green  (8)                                           106
Mariam Quraishi  (11)                                       107
Rémy Cabache  (10)                                          107


## St Katharine's Knockholt CE (A) Primary School, Knockholt

Alice Copeland  (9)                                         107
Emily Hinchcliffe  (10)                                     108
Charlie McKechnie  (9)                                      108
Amy Callaghan  (10)                                         109
Joe Copeland  (10)                                          109
Ruby Cooper  (10)                                           110
Emily Smith  (10)                                           110
Joshua John Walker  (9)                                     110
Kirsty Tapsell  (10)                                        111
Ben Charman  (10)                                           111
Cameron Essam  (11)                                         111
Keturah Paice  (9)                                          112
Daisy Bell  (10)                                            112
Peter Roper  (10)                                           112
Jessica Hudson  (10)                                        113
Tilly Johnson  (10)                                         113
Indianna Bareham  (10)                                      113
William McLoughlin  (10)                                    114
Alexander Rogers  (10)                                      114
George Harber  (10)                                         114
Ben McKechnie  (11)                                         114
Jak Colley  (9)                                             115
Olivia Harbard  (10)                                        115
Emma Pound  (9)                                             116
Sam Link  (10)                                              116
Emma-Louise Richardson  (10)                                117
James Robins  (10)                                          117
Sarah Pickering  (10)                                       118
Daniel Waldron  (11)                                        118

# The Poems

# Fun

Fun is the colour orange, like a sweet in its wrapper,
Fun looks like getting mucky, like mushy peas all down you,
Fun reminds me of plays, like pantomimes in the winter,
Fun tastes like Coke, like all the fizz bubbling in your mouth,
Fun sounds like people screaming, like people on the fast
roller coasters,
Fun feels like winning the favourite fact for Friday,
Like getting something out of the box.

**Matthew Oliver  (11)**
Grace School


# Happiness

Happiness is so nice it makes you want to play.
It feels like a swelling balloon inside you.
It makes you think of bright colours.
It sounds like a new stream gurgling down a hill.
It smells like a chocolate birthday cake.
It tastes like your favourite foods.
It looks like a beautiful valley with green grass and blue streams.
I love being happy.
Don't you?

**Eleana-Jayne Davey  (8)**
Grace School


# My Holly Poem

The holly is prickly and smooth.
It hangs roughly onto the tree, drenched in snow.
The berries dripping with ice like blood
Falling to the swollen ground like bullets.
The prickly leaf is a cactus in a maze.
Behind the flaming meteors are the leaf's swords.

**Alex Gregan**
Great Chart Primary School

# Fireworks

Under the gleaming moon a bolt of screamers rip the inky sky
                       in two pieces.
Through the dim hedge the warm rocket shoots like a python in
                       the deep sky.
Above raucous the rippling fountain comes down like killer raindrops.
Next to the young children their sparklers spring into the shaded
                       midnight sky.
Behind the jingling screamers the rumbling bonfire goes up in flares.
Over the frosty hills the pounding Roman candle bleaches
                       the gloomy sky into cream.
Among the deep hedge the whizzing rocket gasps.
Blasting screamers burst into the glum sky.
Through the coal-black tree the rainbow rocket ripples in
                       the murky sky.

**Tim Williams  (9)**
**Great Chart Primary School**


# Bonfire Night

As whistling screamers explode above my head
the crowd light sparklers and think about what happens next.
Then a frail burst of light sails silently above everybody's heads
and shrills into a sprinkle of light.
A never-ending fountain of light brightens the gloomy sky.
As a Roman candle lifts the crowd's spirits
the rising fire glows brighter and brighter.
Then a J-55 Mustang rocket shoots up in the air
and sprinkles a shining green and red.
As a sparkler zigzags into the air it explodes above the fire.
A Catherine wheel spits out green, red, gold and blue
all over the inky gloom of the night.
Above an old oak tree, tinged flaring stars, spike the bubbly mist
as a Roman candle goes boom above my head.

**Oliver Lawrence  (9)**
**Great Chart Primary School**

# Persephone - Summer

The gleaming petals spring up as she walks through
the forest of unhappiness.

Fragrant orange bubbles shake off the jade branch as
Persephone walks past.

As she skips through the archway of sweet-smelling roses
they change to honey.

The soundless wind travels around Persephone
and causes her cream dress to sway from side to side.

The indigo stream whispers to her as she twirls past
the silky fishes swimming in the water.

The sunlight beams down on Persephone as she glides across
the grassy footpath.

The birds start to twitter and sing as she swoops around
the green forest.

**Daniel Smith  (10)**
**Great Chart Primary School**


# Persephone

It is summer and the flowers and the shimmering grass are sprouting.
The flickering sun is rising very slowly.
All the fluttering butterflies melt in the grassy meadows.
The flushing grapes swell off the tree.
The bitter apple is gleaming in the powerful sun.
The lemon, ever so sharp, resting as the day goes by.
All the oranges are on fire.
When Persephone walks flowers shoot behind her.
She has long hair, all gold and silky.
The red seeded strawberry swirls round and round.
The scented plums peel in the sunny sky.

**Katie Ostridge  (9)**
**Great Chart Primary School**

# Persephone Poem

As Persephone walks by, the beautiful spring blossoms at the touch
of her foot

Her winter footprints are quickly washed away by the jade,
emerald petals

The fresh green grass welcomes her back with a soft grassy whisper

Persephone travels round the world happily exchanging winter
for spring

The juicy apples appear as Persephone's sweet toes grasp the floor

Her black dark hair from the underworld (Hell) turned into bright
sparkling blonde

Persephone's eyes hurt as now she is seeing sunshine and Hades'
Palace draws nearer
Her time in the underworld had come to a close

Persephone has nightmares about returning to Hades and the
telltale gardener.

**Glen Hothersall (10)**
**Great Chart Primary School**


# Persephone

At the beginning of summer, the dazzling sun is warming
his long-lasting hot battery.
The golden, iron apricot flies down to the ground with a flame from
off the heat.
The smell of an orchard makes the glossy plums ripe.
As Persephone walks on the meadow, warm growing flowers dance
in the wind.
The smell is like perfume,
Swirling swiftly to the lime ground.
The blood-red strawberries sparkle in the sunset.

**Megan Katie Pearson (10)**
**Great Chart Primary School**

# An Artist In The Christmas Stable

The barn is as copper as soil on the ground.
Rough sketched hay scattered all around the buff barn,
Smudged aquamarine lies on the pale canvas,
Mary's face is as sparkling stars and as glistening as the
twilight moon.
Murky chocolate coat sits on the pale light man's body,
The man's eyes are as dark as the night sky and the twinkling stars.
Shepherds running to the charcoal stable to find the newborn
baby Jesus,
Jesus cries and cries as they come into the cold stable.
Shepherds bring woolly sheep and leave them outside,
Men riding half bare camels to bring presents to Jesus and to see
Mary and Joseph,
Barn owls hooting, doves squawking, sheep going baa baa
and donkeys eoor, eoo.
Angels glowing on the dull barn next to the twinkling stars.

**Amy Thomas  (10)**
**Great Chart Primary School**

# Persephone

Persephone dances on lush jade grass as the strawberry
petals bloom.
Fragrant plums tingle in the dazzling sun.
Lambs gallop in the sweet-smelling meadows among the golden,
pearly apples.
Expanding stains blush in the melting corn while sandy birds sing.
Blood cherries swirl in the breathing air.
Scented crocuses burst into life as Persephone's dainty
footsteps pass.
Acid splashes drop onto perfumed seeds.
Wax bananas frolic about on their bouncy, luscious leaves.
Buttery butterflies leap from corn to flowers.
Bitter bubbles sway in the refreshing breeze.

**Eleanor Pang  (9)**
**Great Chart Primary School**

# Fireworks

The dazzle whizzes through the sky and spits out rainbow rain.
Under the zooming rocket, a spiky fountain spills freely in
                                        the inky sky.
The star sparkler pinches the frosty cloud made by bullets
                                        shooting from guns.
Among the grey cloud a screamer shooting into nowhere.
An endless lightning flash of a rocket burns the charcoal
                                        darkness and moon.
A sudden crackle creates a shivering fizz making a beautiful star
                                        in the sizzling air.
The war boom from a cannon sounds like a B-17 bomber plane's
                                        bomb landing.
A Catherine wheel uncurls its beam that it has held in.
Overtaking the loudest firework the spitting screamer fires rainbow
                                        stars making a burst of light.
The ear-splitting sound helps you enjoy the 5th of November.
The distant blast make me excited that a waxy Roman candle is
                        on the way for booming the black, grey, soot sky.
The display brightens up the dull 5th of November immensely
                                        and the cloudy sky.

**Ashley Buckman  (9)**
Great Chart Primary School


# Fireworks Poem

A vivid rocket brilliantly shoots up into the resplendent sky.
The twinkling Catherine wheel rotates in the inky sky.
Under the booming midnight sky the shooting Roman candle
fizzles and pops like bacon and eggs under the grill.
When fireworks explode first they look like a very big umbrella
but then dissolve into little tiny ballerinas falling to the ground.
Smoking sparklers shoot out their tiny balls of fire into the misty air.

**Megan McHugh**
Great Chart Primary School

# The Winter Gift

Breaking the midnight's silence,
the ivory prickly stars whisper quietly in the shadowy mist.
They dance wildly, twirling and twisting,
creasing the fine gloom of darkness.
The milky cheese moon lifts from its blurry smoked place in the air,
catching and slicing the ebony coal sky,
then drops it on the solid grassy earth.
The crescent catches a dreamy bundle of thorny stars,
one by one, in a rich net of gold.
Carrying the gathering of stars,
he places them on a blanket of tissue paper.
Creasing the magnificent curtain around the stellar flock,
the shining globe makes a cocoon of stars.
The collection of stars makes a faded shape
of five-sided jagged needles.
The moon gives the gift to you
and leaves it in your Christmas stocking.

**Rhianna Derosa  (9)**
Great Chart Primary School


# Teasel

The tanned gashing teasel slices the night sky,
The narrow spears hack into a fly's body.
The midnight bullets sprinkle onto the bronze soil,
Above the rounded pearly tusks a razor-sharp goblet crouches
                                                    in a ball,
Carving to an emerald-green fly the egg-headed teasel plants
                                                    its next kill.

**Keiran Clifford  (10)**
Great Chart Primary School

# A Spell For Protection Against Evil

To protect yourself from evil you need to find a wish feather
and plant it on top of the Golden Mountain.

Once you have done that you need to catch magic dust
and put it in your pocket to keep evil away.

Next you need to fly to your unicorn to sparkle heaven
and collect five stars and bring them to dream clouds
and place them in the middle.

After you have done that, go to the tree of wonder
and grab three leaves then put them in Ripple River.

Then go to Swirl Moon and snatch seven silver balls.
After then go to shine sun and plant the silver balls.
Collect six golden balls and plant them on Swirl Moon.

The last step is to go to the magic garden
and take the magic crystal, put it in a jar.
That is how to protect yourself from evil.

**Liane Castle  (10)**
**Great Chart Primary School**


# Holly

The emerald prickly leaf delicately glides down to the angel
                                                    white snow.

The scarlet polished marble dangles from the verdant curling tree.

As the fat shiny fire-red pea bounces down the milky covered snow
the shiny smooth leaf enjoys the frosty wind as it rushes through
                                                    its silk cover.

**Jada Atakpo  (10)**
**Great Chart Primary School**

# Fireworks

Among the raining screamers the purring moon rubs
against the dazzling burning flames.
Up and up the tinted shade goes with a rainbow-stained glitter
with the gleaming air by its side.
Under the flickering moon fiery sparks zigzag
with crackles and hisses.
Against the charcoal clouds the inky sky hides
beneath the amazing sparks and spitting showers.
Above the mighty cloud fuzzy lightning
flies up with thunder and colourful rain.
In front of the gates shimmering splashes of paint
zoom in all directions, behind the tall thin trees
the sizzling sparkles crash into space.
Through the ebony night goes the fountain
and then the dancer dips down to the ground
with fading tinges like a butterfly
and disappears in the sooty grass.

**Anissa Boughrarou  (9)**
Great Chart Primary School

# Persephone

Bubbling apples sweeten in a perfumed field.
Laughing petals melting in flaming fields with birds fluttering
in the sky.
The hollow blue sky sparkles above the warm fields full of corn.
Crispy forest melting in a grass field coming to life.
Hollow bananas shining in a field with flowers.
A bright meadow expanding in the woolly sky.
Glass strawberries dazzling in a field of flowers.
Sparkling grapes reddening in a field of grass.
Jade apricots warming in the fragrant sun.
Sparkling lemons bursting in a sandy field.

**Ben Barker  (10)**
Great Chart Primary School

# A Spell For Protection Against Evil

Two golden music notes from a feathered owl,
Fly into the heavenly sky and place them on a silent cloud.
Take a jar of blackberry mist, dream you're a poppy flying through
the moonlight on a jewelled sky.
Grab one of the rippled flowers on the mountaintop and put it in the jar
with the mist.
Then take a feather from a lovebird and put it in your jar.
Take your jar and place it on the scarlet hills.
Say the words *'Evil will never hurt me in good or bad . . .'*

**Antonia Costa (10)**
Great Chart Primary School


# My Best Friend Lizzy

*(Inspired by 'The Writer of this Poem' by Roger McGough)*

My best friend Lizzy is as . . .
Funny as our teacher
As weird as the writer of this poem
As silly as a clown being stupid in front of a crowd
As short as a brown mouse running from a cat
As cheeky as a monkey showing off at the zoo
As graceful as a swan gliding through a lake
As sweet as a strawberry covered in cream and sugar going
into my mouth

As clever as Einstein inventing things
As pretty as a movie star with her make-up
She is as friendly as a star shining on you
As loyal as perfect Peter making a promise
As nice as chocolate in my watering mouth
As busy as a bee rushing to make honey
As drunk as a funky monkey in a pub
She has hazel eyes like an emerald.

**Elena Jamison (8)**
Herne Bay County Junior School

# The Friend Of The Writer Of This Poem

*(Inspired by 'The Writer of this Poem' by Roger McGough)*

The friend of the writer of this poem has
Eyes like two crystal-clear pools of brown.
She is as friendly as the BFG at Christmas with little Sophie.
She loves to read her magazine till she gets the next series.
She loves to save animals and if one of her friends are hurt she'll
go and help them.
She has such lovely brown hair, kind of long but kind of short.
She's taller than me; probably three quarters the size of my teacher.
She is as beautiful as a super model on the catwalk.
She is as clever as a grey dolphin performing tricks.
My best friend Is Lily McCabe.

**Paige Tilbrook  (9)**
**Herne Bay County Junior School**

# The Bully

'I'm better than you,' a bully started to sneer,
*This can't be happening*, I started to fear.
'You're smaller than me, you're a little worm,'
At that moment I started to squirm.
'Don't think that you can get away,
I'm bigger than you, I'll make you stay.'
I couldn't move, I was beaten,
If he was a lion I'd be eaten.
This happens nearly every day,
All my happiness just wastes away.
My courage always lets me down,
Especially when I see him in town.
My mum thinks he is my friend,
She does not know it's all pretend.

**Leah Thompson  (9)**
**Herne Bay County Junior School**

# My Mum Is . . .

My mum is as happy as a cat drinking smooth white milk
as funny as a grey elephant flying in the sky
as slim as a dictionary sitting on a desk
as busy as a bee collecting honey on every flower in the field
as tidy as my grandad cleaning the dustbin out every day.

**Chloe Compton (8)**
Herne Bay County Junior School


# Holly Is . . .

As clever as Miss Smith when she is teaching us
as thin as a skeleton running
as slow as a green tortoise
as short as a brown rat
as happy as a running horse
as funny as a clown telling jokes
as busy as my mum when she is tidying the house
as helpful as my dad when he is in the mood
as gentle as Mrs Ashby
as silly as a funny monkey eating bananas in a tree.

**Nicole Redford (8)**
Herne Bay County Junior School


# My Dog Is . . .

My dog is as . . .
cute as a mouse playing happily
spotty as a leopard
as lovely as a mother kissing you
as fast as a cheetah running after a nice juicy deer
cuddly as a ginormous bear
blue eyes like the night ocean water
as lazy as my dad
good at keeping me happy.

**Harry Moody-Smith (8)**
Herne Bay County Junior School

# My Dad

My dad is . . .
As fast as striking lightning,
As strong as the oak tree in the middle of the forest,
As tall as an old cottage near the forest,
As greedy as Horrid Henry stealing sweets,
As perfect as Perfect Peter doing maths,
As moody as Moody Margaret playing the trumpet loudly,
As hungry as a chick clucking for food in the morning before
the sun rose.

**Gobi Sriram  (9)**
Herne Bay County Junior School


# My Family

I think my sister is a pea because she drinks lots of tea
I think my mum is a gorilla because she wants a caterpillar
I think my dad is a key because he makes lots of coffee
I think my cousin is a table because he has wireless cable
I think my nan has blonde hair because she met a polar bear
I think my grandad does not care because he has no hair
I think my auntie is a dog because she likes to snog
I think my second cousin is a chair because he ate a pear.

**Tom Elliott  (9)**
Herne Bay County Junior School


# My Mum Is . . .

As funny as a huge elephant doing ballet
as busy as a bee collecting nectar
as angry as a hungry crocodile
as slim as a kind fish
as happy as a happy clown
as small as a tiny pencil
as kind as a licking dog
as cuddly as my softest teddy bear.

**Amy Simson  (8)**
Herne Bay County Junior School

# The Writer's Friend Of This Poem

*(Inspired by 'The Writer of this Poem' by Roger McGough)*

The writer's friend of this poem is . . .
as funny as a humorous clown cycling and juggling
as mean as humongous King Kong in a bad mood
as happy as a soft chilled-out cat in the burning sun
as brunette as chocolate oozing in the hot fire
as clever as William Shakespeare working hard in his studies
as gentle as a furry, fluffy feather falling to the ground
as beautiful as a model on the catwalk with all her make-up
as strong as a unique individual star in the midnight sky
as fast as a fire engine zooming through a long street
and my best friend is Paige Tilbrook.

**Lily McCabe  (9)**
Herne Bay County Junior School

# The Vain Old Man

The old town of Farlin,
Lay fast asleep,
For its darkness fell upon the sky,
Silent as a mouse.

Within a house of light,
A vain old man stood,
Gazing into a mirror,
With all his eyes' energy.

No sound came from the house,
As he died with pain,
The glass shattered splintering him,
With a thousand tiny pieces.

It was a mystery,
How he had died,
Since the people of the town,
Were afraid to think the truth.

**Megan Jones  (10)**
Lady Joanna Thornhill Primary School

# The Treasure

The treasure lay untouched,
In a damp, cold cave,
Waves lapped on the treasure chest,
Spreading gold coins far and wide.
The sound of children shouting,
Disturbed the silence of the waters.
Then a chink of metal or gold, urged them closer.
A shout echoed around for miles it seemed,
As one of the children picked up a gold coin . . .

**Jemima Barnes (9)**
**Lady Joanna Thornhill Primary School**


# Snow

The morning sun revealed the heavenly icy feathers,
floating silently on the wind and settling on an unprotected tree.
The red robin sang among the drifting flakes,
dancing in the sky, magically cooling the already chilled air,
before falling gently to the welcoming ground.
Delighted children made snow angels and listened to the crunch
of the snow.

**Emily Coyne**
**Langton Green CP School**


# Snow

Gently melting, the snow greets his friend below.
Softly, secretly, the snow meets the cold damp floor.
Scattering, tempting, the snow finds a home.
Laying, melting, the snow turns into water.
White, fun snow is being played by young happy children.
Cold snow turns to water which children play and jump in.

**Rhianna Steer (11)**
**Langton Green CP School**

# Snow

Flaky showers of feathery snow quickly but silently drift to the ground.
Blissfully, chilling snow glides to the freezing ground.
Drifting, gracefully the ice-cold snow falls to the ground.

**James Wakelin**
Langton Green CP School

# Snow

Slowly, calmly the snow falls on the rooftop
Silently, slowly the snow falls like feathers on the rooftop

Slowly, the damp snow falls on the rooftop
Silently, the ignorant snow hovers down on the rooftops

Slowly the snow drifts on me!

**Ryan Searle  (10)**
Langton Green CP School

# Sugar Snow

Blanketing, heavenly, gracefully like sugar snow
Snowing heavenly through frosting air
Filtering calmly, slowly it goes
Fading quietly nobody knows.

**Ella Davey**
Langton Green CP School

# Snow

Melting gently to the soft platform
Scattering softly to the cold ground
Laying gently to the hard ground
Freezing cold soft snowflakes drifting onto me.

**Bethany Noble**
Langton Green CP School

# Let It Snow!

Calmly, quietly, the snowflakes drift in the sky,
Freezing slowly, white fluffy balls fall,
Frosty cold lumps of snow, start to create a snowman,
Chilling silently, the wet blanket of snow fades away,
Exciting fun, sadly comes to an end.

**Kate Murphy**
Langton Green CP School


# What Am I?

I have pointy ears, I say miaow,
I'm much smaller than a cow,
I like to play with lots of mice,
They are really yummy and really nice.
I have four paws and twenty claws.
I'm allowed out in the dark,
The thing I'm scared of has a bark.
I like playing in the garden chasing any butterfly,
What am I?

**Abigail Teresa Fitzgerald (7)**
Long Mead Community Primary School


# Benny

My pet is the best pet yet.
My cat is named Benny and he has a girlfriend named Penny.
My pet is the best pet yet.
He has a big round head and he sleeps on my bed.
If he has the flu he will cuddle you.
My pet is the best pet yet.
He is always fat while I put on a hat.
He has a brother called ginger
And he had an injury on his knee.
My pet is the best pet yet.

**Jessie Anderson (8)**
Long Mead Community Primary School

# My Poem About My Rabbit

There he was my rabbit
He jumps about all day like a bad habit
We call him Fluffy
But really he should have been called Scuffy

He likes to lay midday in the sun
Oh he's my little bun
He is a little hun

He has his food with a *munch munch munch*
Then a carrot with a crunch *crunch crunch*

Well it's come to the end of the day for my bun
So now he goes to sleep
Kept nice and warm by his nice clean hay
Oh bless my little hun.

**Damian Hammett (8)**
**Long Mead Community Primary School**


# Sasha

My kitten is very nice
But she keeps catching mice
She is grey and white
Doesn't hiss, scratch or bite
At night she plays with my dog Ben
While I'm sleeping in bed at ten
She wakes me up by purring
Won't stop while I'm stirring
She sits on my dad's lap
Eats loads of food to get fat
Once a kitten, now a cat.

**Crystal Dobson (7)**
**Long Mead Community Primary School**

# Rabbits

Rabbits are sweet
Rabbits are cute
All dressed up in a big fluffy suit.

**Jessica Tapp  (7)**
Long Mead Community Primary School


# Jealousy

Jealousy is the colour of a dark red demon ready to dominate its fear.
Jealousy smells like scorching steam rummaging through your nose.
Jealousy looks like you're surrounded by the dangers of hell that
haunt you for all eternity.
Jealousy feels like a new and overtaking person is trying to release
itself out of your soul.
Jealousy sounds like a royal funeral running around your head.
Jealousy tastes like a sour lemon's taste that is everlasting.
Jealousy reminds me of me when I was the best at something,
But some person had to snatch that from me.

**Thomas Hallett  (10)**
Lympne CE Primary School


# Sadness

Sadness is blue like the bright wide sky on a clear day
Sadness looks like an old abandoned house on an empty street
Sadness tastes like the bitter taste of the ocean waves
Sadness sounds like the gentle soft wind on a calm, calm night
Sadness feels like the cold water of a river running down your spine.

**Ethan Charles Dunlop Wright  (9)**
Lympne CE Primary School

# Jealousy

Jealousy is red like an explosive volcano pouring out lava,
Sounds like pumice stones beating at your heart,
It tastes like red-hot chilli pepper erupting in your mouth,
It smells like the rotting bodies in Hell,
It looks like a genie who's been let loose from his chains,
It reminds me of a boiling kettle ready to send out its hot vapour,
hot and steamy.

**Harry Gibbons (10)**
Lympne CE Primary School


# Fear

Fear is grey like smoke out of a burning fire.
Fear sounds like people all scared and crying from a crowd.
It tastes like smoke trying to cough up from your throat.
It smells like horror and makes you panic.
Fear looks like a burning building of uneasiness.
Fear feels like a worry inside your body.
It reminds me of our school burning down to ashes.

**Megan King (8)**
Lympne CE Primary School


# Anger

Anger is red like the Devil himself,
It sounds like Hell's thunder,
It tastes like the hottest red-hot chilli pepper,
It smells like the spiciest curry,
It looks like the most evil beast ever,
It feels like your body's stopped working,
It reminds me of mayhem underground.

**William Foster (10)**
Lympne CE Primary School

# Jealousy

Jealousy is green like a glistening emerald lighting up the sky,
As the seaweed swirls up above the water banks.
It tastes so revolting if you swallow great big mouthfuls.
Feels like a new beginning catching the corner of my eye
                                    playing a game of eye spy.
The sea sounds like breaking glass crashing on my kitchen floor.
The sea is a horrible salty flower, I never want to gulp it down.
The sea looks like a tap that has been on for hours and
                                    overflowing the sink.
The sea reminds me of a globe ball being shaken up.

**Francesca Storti  (8)**
Lympne CE Primary School


# Love

The colour of love is a light pink shining in the sky.
Love sounds like your heart pumping a million times a second.
Love tastes like a marshmallow melting in your mouth.
Love looks like your favourite song being sung to you.
Love smells like blood-red roses growing their thorns.
Love feels like having a hot bubbly bath.
Love reminds you of a boyfriend blowing you a kiss.

**Emily King  (10)**
Lympne CE Primary School


# Happiness

Happiness is pink like a dragon trying to look sweet.
It sounds like an aeroplane flying through the air.
It tastes like chocolate melting on my tongue.
It smells like bright red berries growing on a bush.
It feels like people touching me making me feel safe.
It looks like people having fun.
It reminds me of when I play with my dad.

**Amy Ruffell  (9)**
Lympne CE Primary School

# Love!

The colour of love is light pink shining in the sky,
Love sounds like your heart pumping one million times a second,
Love tastes like a marshmallow melting in your mouth,
Love looks like your favourite song being sung to you,
Love smells like blood-red roses growing their thorns,
Love feels like having a hot bubble bath,
Love reminds me of your boyfriend blowing a kiss.

**Phoebe Bruford  (10)**
Lympne CE Primary School

# Jealousy

Jealousy is red like the Demon's protruding eyes
Jealousy sounds like funeral music
Jealousy tastes like the cold blood of the Demon
Jealousy smells like the rotting souls in Hell
Jealousy looks like a poisonous Texas rattlesnake
Jealousy feels like someone stealing your soul.

**Sam Hindess  (10)**
Lympne CE Primary School

# Happiness

Happiness is like the powder blue of a summer sky
It feels like a summer morning when you can do anything
It smells like a chocolate fountain overflowing
It reminds me of a day out with my family
Happiness looks like a shiny new football just waiting to be kicked
It sounds like all the birds waking up in spring
Happiness is a beautiful birthday cake, the best you could ever have.

**Frank Morgan  (9)**
Lympne CE Primary School

# Anger

Anger is red like lava rushing from the centre of the Earth.
Anger reminds me of the Earth shaking when earthquakes happen.
Anger looks like the Devil dancing round the gravestones.
It tastes like a poisoned Christmas cake.
It feels like you're starving to death.
Anger sounds like thunder hitting the Earth.
Anger smells like a sewer full of rats.

**Robert Leigh (8)**
Lympne CE Primary School

# Love

Love is green like the grass rolling down the hills.
It smells like perfume around me.
It sounds like getting a merit, everyone clapping.
It feels all warm and cosy.
It reminds me of being at home, with everyone I love.
Love tastes like a chocolate mousse in a pink love heart box.
It looks like a heart that is precious.

**James Wood (11)**
Lympne CE Primary School

# Anger

Anger is red like the fires of Hell.
It smells like burning rubber for racing cars.
It sounds like a teacher blowing her whistle.
It tastes like red-hot chillies.
It feels like your veins are going to burst.
It reminds me of all the bad things I have done (bad).
It looks like the world is all against you!

**Cameron McKay (10)**
Lympne CE Primary School

# Hate

Hate is black like the sky going together and making a hurricane.
It looks like a wet and windy day.
It tastes like bitter lemon with a mouldy orange in it.
It reminds me of a friend that betrays me and says stuff
                                    behind my back.
It smells like manure spread over the fields on a hot day.
It sounds like cars screeching then a burning mist in the air.
It feels like a hot kettle's been thrown over you.

**Rebecca Phillips (11)**
Lympne CE Primary School


# Love

Love is red like on Valentine's Day.
It reminds me of red roses in a vase.
It feels like happiness.
It looks like a heart thumping up and down.
It tastes like a sweet taste of watermelon.
It sounds like the honeybees collecting pollen up from flowers.
It smells like a rose.

**James Pearcy (11)**
Lympne CE Primary School


# Love

Love is pink like a row of lilies in the beautiful sunset.
It sounds like a peaceful song.
It tastes like chocolate melting in your mouth.
It feels like you have goosebumps all over.
It smells like a mix of the best flowers ever.
It looks like the best thing you have ever seen.
It reminds me of the sunniest day ever.
Love comes from the bottom of your heart.

**Olivia Boutwood (8)**
Lympne CE Primary School

# Happiness

Happiness is the colour of bright white.
It feels like you are not alone,
It feels like happiness takes you all the way.
Happiness reminds me of all my friends and family.
Happiness makes me feel like I am lying down on the White Cliffs
of Dover.
Happiness smells like one thousand strawberries.
Happiness looks like a field of your friends cheering me on.
It sounds like your friends saying you are a good friend.

**Sean Wythe  (8)**
**Lympne CE Primary School**


# Love

Love is a light red like someone's lips.
Love sounds like bluebirds singing over the White Cliffs of Dover.
Love tastes like sweet chicken.
Love smells like newborn puppies.
Love looks like a rainbow of hearts.
Love reminds me of happiness.

**Jack Bryant  (9)**
**Lympne CE Primary School**


# Anger

Anger is bright red like warm blood.
It reminds me of death.
It tastes like salt.
It sounds like a million drums pumping.

**Jake Edwards  (8)**
**Lympne CE Primary School**

# Anger Is My Thing

Anger is red like the Devil.
Anger smells like some rotten cheese.
The sound is like a herd of elephants.
It looks like a big red ball of fur.
It tastes like some hot chilli sauce.
It feels like a broken nerve.
Anger reminds me how much my friends are nasty to me.

**Abigail Cole  (9)**
Lympne CE Primary School


# Love Is Pure

Love is pink as rose
And feels like the most enchanting place in your heart.
It reminds you of an act of marriage
And smells like the air of a kiss.
It tastes like strawberries.
It looks like two people on a honeymoon.

**Ambre Lelievre  (8)**
Lympne CE Primary School


# Hate

Hate is orange like an orange.
It reminds me of the army.
It smells like soot.
It sounds like people marching.
It feels like snow.
It looks like tears.
It tastes like steel.

**Callum Kilby  (9)**
Lympne CE Primary School

# Happiness

Happiness is a sign of kindness and truthful people around you
and for everyone in the world.
Happiness is the colour of calm colours like pinks, purples
and light blue.
Happiness is not just what you say to people, it is what you do
to people as well.
Happiness tastes like a soft and gentle skin of a plum.
Happiness smells like a sweet strawberry you've just picked.
Happiness looks like a million hearts floating in the sky.
Happiness feels like you have a friend beside you all the time.

**Jessica Thorpe-Young  (9)**
Lympne CE Primary School


# Funny

It's like neon blue,
It sounds like a clown honking his horn,
It tastes like egg and bacon,
Smells of strawberries and cream,
Looks like your friends doing funny things,
Feels weird and likeable,
It reminds me of a gorilla scratching his head.

**Aaron Norris  (11)**
Lympne CE Primary School


# Sadness

Sadness is blue like a whale
That's been under the sea for a thousand years.
Sadness tastes like the saltiest sea.
It sounds like someone screeching.

**Lewis Wiles  (9)**
Lympne CE Primary School

# Fear

Fear is grey like a mist that strangles anyone.
Fear sounds like a screaming bullet heading for a German.
Fear tastes like dog's liver on mayonnaise left in the sun for a week.
Fear smells like a chicken's sick that has eaten an eyeball.
Fear looks like a ghost with a bleeding tongue.
Fear feels like blood has frozen with fright.
Fear reminds me of when a man pointed a gun at my mum's head.

**Owen McLean (8)**
Lympne CE Primary School

# Anger

Anger tastes like someone eating lava.
Anger smells like 1,000 power stations around you.
Anger looks like the sun exploding.
Anger is as light as one thousand suns.
Anger sounds like 100 cars exploding.
Anger is the colour of blood.
Anger makes you feel like smashing your head on a wall.

**Charles Jason Watson (9)**
Lympne CE Primary School

# Happiness

Happiness is like a rainbow.
It's when people called angels sing.
Sweet taste of watering apples.
Smells like cookies coming out of an oven.
Walking out of the house and seeing roses.
It feels like Heaven.

**Alice Andrews**
Lympne CE Primary School

# Love

Love is like pure blood flowing through your head.
Love looks like you're in a peaceful place where people are
kind to you.
It's like you're going to die in a garden.
The colour is white, pure white in a peaceful house.
It smells like pure roses flowing through the air.
It sounds like fresh sun brightening up the Earth.
It feels like the Earth quiet for the whole day.

**Ellie Burch  (8)**
Lympne CE Primary School


# Love

Love is pink dreams in the mind.
Love tastes like bubblegum.
Love sounds like calm music.
Love smells like a dark chocolate.
Love looks like pretty, beautiful fuchsias in the air.
Love feels like glitter flying in the house.
Love reminds me of sparkles of stars in the pure sky.

**Sophie Parker  (8)**
Lympne CE Primary School


# Love

It feels like something good is going round your body,
The colour is like the red hot sun is beaming,
It smells like pure rose flowing in the air,
It sounds so quiet as if nothing is in the air,
It tastes like roses.

**Lauren Newland  (9)**
Lympne CE Primary School

# Happiness

The colour of happiness is beautiful bright red like the colour of a rose.
Also the smell is almost like a big juicy strawberry.
It could almost feel like the wind blowing in your eyes.
The look is pink flesh and it could also look shy
And it could sound like a thumping heart.
The taste is like some purple blueberries hanging on a tree.

**Elisabeth Devine  (10)**
Lympne CE Primary School

# Fear

Fear is the colour black,
Black as coal, black as soot from a volcano.
Fear tastes like sour fruit melting and stinging your mouth.
Fear feels like sharp knives pressing against your skin.
Fear looks like a black shadow chasing behind you.
Fear sounds like a thing you don't know creeping up on you.

**Elizabeth Nash  (9)**
Lympne CE Primary School

# Jealousy

Jealousy is green like a glistening emerald lighting up the sky,
It makes all the things I like taste nasty or go bitter.
Looks like seaweed whirring and whistling round and round,
Sounds like grass shimmering in the sun.
It feels like water so slippery and salty
And reminds me of shells, coal and all the living creatures
                                                    around me.

**Courtney Jade Hawkins  (9)**
Lympne CE Primary School

# Anger

Anger is like a vampire biting your arm
And you feel like you're going to explode.
It smells like rotten cheese and gone-off eggs.
Orange is anger.
It is nice and bright and it tastes sour or of a dark satsuma
                                         and it's colourful.
It reminds me of a fatal car crash where someone's died.
It sounds like a bomb going *bang!*
And tastes like drinking blood.

**Connor Jenkins  (8)**
Lympne CE Primary School


# Fear Is . . .

Fear is black like a violent, aggressive and dark
                              desolated wilderness.
Fear feels like you are being sucked down by an angry plughole
                              with no one to save you.
Fear sounds like you are in the middle of wolves howling
                              in the woods.
Fear reminds you of being lost in darkness.
Fear tastes like you are eating black smoke suffocating you.
Fear smells like the worst food in the world.

**Adam Pringle  (10)**
Lympne CE Primary School


# Anger

Anger is a red colour like a volcano erupting.
It sounds like a kettle whistling.
Anger tastes as sour as a lemon.
It looks like a red devil exploding.
It feels as hot as lava.
Anger reminds me of the sun!

**Gemma Archer  (8)**
Lympne CE Primary School

# Ready . . . Steady . . . Go!

When you've won a race
Don't you want to freeze
This time in your mind?
You don't want to forget
The clapping and the cheering
The happiness around you
You'll feel that warm glow
Inside your stomach
The buzzing in your head
You feel like you're getting
Bigger and bigger
The fame and fortune
But getting that medal
Wow! That's the best bit
But don't forget
That photo shoot
To go in the papers!
But don't forget
It's only sports day!

**Naomi Clarke**
Lympne CE Primary School


# Happiness

Happiness is the loving colour of the rainbow that shines every day,
Happiness is the sound like angels calling from Heaven above,
Happiness tastes soft and gentle like the skin of a plum,
Happiness smells like a newly grown rose,
Happiness looks like a ray of sunshine shining through my window,
Happiness feels like a satsuma oozing in my mouth,
Happiness reminds me of the good times in my life.

**Samantha Wagland**
Lympne CE Primary School

# Happiness Poem

Happiness is like a million daisies
swooping down from the sky.

Also hearts and daffodils
with a scorching beaming and boiling sun
just saying 'happiness is the best emotion'.

Having picnics all day,
going to the beach
and having a wonderful happy time.

When you go from all happiness
you feel like you shouldn't be sad
and go back to happiness.
So *be happy!*

Happiness tastes like
you're being loved by relatives
and all your friends,
playing and having fun.

It smells like summer has come
when it is winter.

**Toby James Neill  (8)**
Lympne CE Primary School

# Happiness

Happiness is like the sun
shining out and flowers everywhere.

It sounds like people being polite and kind.

It is like the smell of roses, daisies and violets.

Happiness looks like life has come back in you and you feel fresh.

Happiness makes you feel proud.

A taste comes in your mouth and you feel fresh.

**Jae Stacey  (8)**
Lympne CE Primary School

# Happiness

I feel the colour of happiness is yellow
For all the nice things in the world are normally yellow like the sun.
The sound of happiness is like angels singing with the birds.
If you listen carefully the birds are there,
But do you dare to go up there in the trees?
The smell of happiness smells like sweet red roses
With girls doing dances and poses.
It tastes like a sweet red strawberry with goodness all mixed up.
It looks like an angel playing on the harp
With sunflowers growing up the path.

**Lilli Coates  (9)**
**Lympne CE Primary School**


# A Joyful Poem

J  oy is happiness, like a sun shining bright,
O  n your face there is a big smile from ear to ear,
Y  our body is in an energetic mood,
F  un and games,
U  nlimited good things will come your way,
L  aughing with your friends,

   Your joy will never end!

**Rosie Gallagher  (10)**
**Lympne CE Primary School**


# Sadness

Sadness to me is a cold droopy blue.
It sounds like water swishing in and out of a cave.
Sadness tastes dull and boring, even a hot chilli pepper.
It looks like grey clouds coming over your life.
Sadness can feel as though the world is caving in.
It smells like a deserted castle.
Sadness reminds me of losing your mum.

**Becky Maynard  (10)**
**Lympne CE Primary School**

# Love

Love is pink like candyfloss,
It sounds like a boat rocking slightly against the calm sea,
It tastes like pineapple juice with a hint of orange,
It smells like perfume in a girl's bedroom,
It looks like melted chocolate,
It feels like a soft cushion rubbing against you,
It reminds me of endless fields of flowers.

**Morwenna James (10)**
Lympne CE Primary School

# Anger

Anger is red like your head's going to explode,
Anger sounds horrible because you shout and scream,
Anger feels bad because you feel annoyed and stressed,
Anger looks scary because your face scrunches up,
Anger reminds me of a volcano exploding.

**Sam Dance (10)**
Lympne CE Primary School

# Happiness

Happiness is pink like a love heart,
It sounds like bells of love,
It tastes like Cadbury's chocolate melting in your mouth,
It smells like lavender scented candles,
It looks like pink dyed pearls,
It feels like brand new smooth card,
It reminds me of Christmas Eve waiting for the morning.

**Katie Millar (11)**
Lympne CE Primary School

# Fear

Fear is purple like the night sky, endless and empty.
Fear sounds like pain, screaming.
Fear tastes like sour grapes, inedible and despicable.
Fear smells like a damp, unlived in house, alone and unusable.
Fear feels like you're alone and you always will be, terror, shame.
Fear reminds you of eternally falling, nothingness, hopeless.
Fear is unthinkable.

**Jacob Burden (10)**
Lympne CE Primary School

# Love

Love is pink like a beautiful picture,
Love sounds like little birds in the trees,
Love tastes like smooth strawberry mousse,
Love smells like sweet perfume,
Love looks like a cloud shaped like a heart,
Love feels like a soft kitten,
Love reminds me of lovely places.

**Ruby Stone (9)**
Lympne CE Primary School

# Love

Love is red like a rose,
Love is quiet like the birds,
Love tastes of chocolate in your mouth,
Love has a sweet scent like a flower,
Love is a heart full of pride,
Love is soft like a cloud,
Love reminds me of my family.

**Robert Gunn (9)**
Lympne CE Primary School

# Love

Love is pink like a bunny's nose,
Love sounds like the soft wind that blows,
Love tastes like chocolates on Valentine's Day,
Love smells like a newborn lamb in the month of May,
Love looks like true love's first kiss,
Love feels like a delightful bliss,
Love reminds me of nice warm toes,
Love reminds me of the sun's warm ray,
Love reminds me of a nice big warm hug.

**Aisha Grover**
**Lympne CE Primary School**


# Love

Love is pink like a beautiful rose,
It sounds like birds tweeting in the morn,
It feels like you're in Heaven and you feel like jelly,
It smells like the aroma of fresh cookies,
It reminds me of laying in the sea,
It tastes like a home-made chocolate cake,
It looks like the most beautiful tulip.

**Oliver Warren  (9)**
**Lympne CE Primary School**


# Love

Love is the colour of red like a heart.
Love sounds like a sunny day.
Love tastes like a roast dinner.
It smells like a rose blossoming.
Love looks like the sun.
Love feels like sucking on a sweet.
It reminds me of romance.

**William Lindsay-Webb  (8)**
**Lympne CE Primary School**

# Fear

Fear is black like the night's darkness,
Fear sounds like goats being killed,
Fear tastes like raw red bloody meat,
Fear looks like the gruesome demons of the dark ages,
Fear feels like sharp, lumpy, hard, gooey skin of a monster,
Fear smells like mushrooms,
Fear reminds me of death - a thing everyone in the
world experiences,
Fear you get before going into battle.

**Barnaby James Apps  (9)**
Lympne CE Primary School


# Happiness

Happiness is purple like bluebells,
Happiness sounds like laughter,
Happiness tastes like the sweet taste of chocolate,
Happiness smells like spring when the flowers grow,
Happiness looks like a smile on everyone's face,
Happiness feels like the softness of snow,
Happiness reminds me of the beach when everyone's having fun.

**Simeon Thorne  (10)**
Lympne CE Primary School


# Love

Love is red like red roses in the garden.
Love sounds like a gentle breeze dancing around.
Love tastes like a warm Sunday dinner.
Love smells like cookies being cooked in the oven.
Love looks like a warm fire glowing in the fireplace.
Love feels like warm hands hugging you.
Love reminds me of a warm summer's day.

**Sophie Miller  (10)**
Lympne CE Primary School

## Anger

Anger is grey like the steam of a train,
It sounds like a scream of terrible pain,
It feels like very cold toes,
It smells like peppermint up your nose,
It looks like a dark sky,
It tastes like rotten blueberry pie,
It reminds me of Africa's terrible strain
And the rareness of beautiful rain.

**Morgen Campbell  (11)**
Lympne CE Primary School


## Love

Love is red like a rose
Love sounds like bunnies rattling through food
Love tastes like strawberries
Love smells like perfume
Love looks like a kitten staring at you
Love feels like a dog jumping up at you
Love reminds me of a loving family.

**Megan Ratcliffe**
Lympne CE Primary School


## Love

Love is red like red roses spread out everywhere.
Love sounds like seagulls squawking.
Love tastes like hot spicy chilli.
Love smells like white washing liquid.
Love looks like a bath of confetti.
Love feels like my family hugging me.
Love reminds me of looking out for friends.

**Emily Harris  (10)**
Lympne CE Primary School

# Happiness

Happiness is cheerful and has the colour of a gleaming rainbow
in the sky.
The sound of happiness is when people smile dazzlingly and laugh
as if they're being entertained lively.
It tastes like pink sparkling cakes baking in the oven.
Happiness smells like cute little angels swooping in the air leaving
the sweet smell of heaven behind them.
It looks like pink flesh and it could also look shy.
It feels like nothing can scare you and you're safe because people
only want peace.
Happiness reminds me of everything that's colourful and you feel
like you're in a bubble, so you're safe.

**Emma Norris  (9)**
Lympne CE Primary School


# Anger

Anger is red like a big raving volcano,
It sounds like an erupting volcano
Ready to lose control any minute now.
It tastes like a hot and spicy pepper
Making you come alive and shout.
It smells like the Devil's fiery breath
Spitting on your face and everything happy
Is wilting away into horrible raving things.
It looks like the Devil with a red-hot stick
And horns so spiky that they burn red fire.
It feels like dark, dirty black smoke coming from your ears,
Loud, deafening train whistles round and round your head.
It reminds me of everything in the world,
Things that nobody can describe.

**Imogen Ellis  (9)**
Lympne CE Primary School

# On A Peaceful Night

On a peaceful night when the pink and gold sheen from the
sleeping sun fades,
On a peaceful night when the moon beams down on the crystal
clear midnight waves,
On a peaceful night a sky-blue unicorn canters through the foam,
On a peaceful night stars twinkle, whispering silently in the darkness
the sky has become,
On a peaceful night flowers close their beautiful petals
and sway gently in the chilling breeze,
On a peaceful night a baby laughs as a wind chime tinkles in
the wind,
On a peaceful night I slumber sweetly, tucked in my bed dreaming
of what the future will bring,
This is my night, peaceful and motionless, until the sun rises again.

**Ellie Cox (11)**
Lympne CE Primary School

# Love

Love is red like a beautiful rose.
Love sounds like a warm breeze blowing through your hair.
Love tastes like a hot chocolate on a Saturday morning.
Love smells like a warm summer's day.
Love looks like roses falling from the sky and exploding
all around you.
Love feels like a scarf wrapped round you with the scent of lavender.
Love reminds me of all the happiness in the world.

**Gwen Ludlow (9)**
Lympne CE Primary School

# Love

Love is pink like clouds in a sunset,
It smells like the smell of rich chocolate,
It looks like a firework at the first gaze,
It feels like you're having an nice warm bath,
It tastes like newly baked bread,
It sounds like a cute kitten miaowing at you,
It reminds you of when you start a fresh, new school year.

**Candice Lelievre (10)**
Lympne CE Primary School

# Happiness

Happiness is yellow like the shining sun,
Happiness sounds like laughing children,
Happiness tastes like fresh meat,
Happiness looks like the setting sun,
Happiness feels like soft cat fur,
Happiness reminds me of God above.

**Paddy Cox (9)**
Lympne CE Primary School

# Love

Love is pink like a lovely pink sky
Love sounds like birds singing
It tastes like my Mum's cooking
It feels like love in the wind
It smells like a new flower
It looks like a baby
It reminds me of sunny days.

**Samuel Day (9)**
Lympne CE Primary School

# The Magic Box

*(Based on 'Magic Box' by Kit Wright)*

I will put in my box . . .

The scent of an overcooked meal
That's just come out of the oven,
The sight of a cheetah chomping on cheese.

I will put in my box . . .

The height of the Eiffel Tower,
Spider-Man's power
And the last word of Queen Victoria.

I will put in my box . . .

The grass on the hills in San Francisco,
The fluff of Annie's hair shining in the night,
The smell of Kylie's perfume
In its beautiful shiny bottle.

I will put in my box . . .

The smell of fishes in the deep blue sea,
Sixty drumsticks for you and me,
Five hundred colours from day and night,
If my box is with me it will be alright.

My box is fashioned with stars and stripes,
With crowns and hats,
Its hinges are made from golden steel
And the rest is sparkling emerald.

I shall fly in my box
Over mountain tops, as I float, as I float
Over mountain tops in the beautiful, beautiful light.

**Summer Woodall  (8)**
**Mundella Primary School**

# The Magic Box

*(Based on 'Magic Box' by Kit Wright)*

I will put into my box . . .

an enormous shop with loads of kids' clothes
a mooing cow in the field
the noise of a singing farmer

I will put into my box . . .

a fish in a brilliant tank
the smell of peanut butter
and the sound of someone humming

I will put into my box . . .

three cute baby seals
a book on beautiful dolphins
and the first word of a baby girl

I will put into my box . . .

four loud fireworks
the noise of a loud stereo
and the swiftness of the water from the tap

My box is fashioned from ice and silver and steel
with loads of moons on the lid and jokes in the corners
its hinges are toe joints of monkeys

I shall sit in my box
while watching a movie called 'Annie'
then eat popcorn on a sunny day
under the colours of the rainbow.

**Kyle Featherbee (9)**
**Mundella Primary School**

# Annie's Magical Box

*(Based on 'Magic Box' by Kit Wright)*

I shall put in my box . . .

The scent of honey from a bee,
The feeling of a pillow on your head at night
And the finest apple from a tree.

I shall put in my box . . .

The sound of a pencil scratching,
The sight of the rainbow's colours
And the crack of an egg hatching.

I shall put in my box . . .

The feel of a fox's fur,
The squeaking of blue dolphins
And a ginger cat's purr.

I shall put in my box . . .

The sizzle of the frying pan,
The horrible feel of goo
And the cooling of a fan.

My box is styled with silver, bronze and gold.
It's fashioned with white stars and spots.
It says 'handle with care' in letters that are bold.

I will float in my box to other lands
Upon the seven seas
And go to beaches with golden sand.

**Annie Blomfield (8)**
**Mundella Primary School**

# The Magic Box

*(Based on 'Magic Box' by Kit Wright)*

I will put into the box . . .
A beach covered in golden sand
A drop of ink from the finest pen
And a flicker of electric from a bulb

I will put into the box . . .
An inch of water from the Atlantic Ocean
The first raindrop from the sky
And the last tear from an eye

I will put into the box . . .
The scent of lavender in a field
A petal from a pink rose
And the colour of a dandelion

I will put into the box . . .
The feeling of happiness
The blazing heat of the sun
And the taste of chocolate

My box is fashioned from diamonds, ice and glass
Its hinges are made from human finger joints
The key is made out of smooth silk and metal.

**Alexander Norman  (8)**
**Mundella Primary School**

# The Magic Box

*(Based on 'Magic Box' by Kit Wright)*

I will put into my box . . .
Eight golden wishes spoken at night
The big ears from a North Pole elf
A big bug that lets through all the light
A chocolate bar that gives me health

I will put into my box . . .
The feel of a vampire's fang
The fourth season of 2007
A spark of a firework bang
A big brother that is now eleven

I will put into my box . . .
The noise of lightning
A Chinese crown
A shark that's frightening
And a dragon's frown

My box is fashioned with blue hearts
Its hinges are the webbed feet of seagulls
Its lid is covered in pink stars with a background of orange

I will fly to the moon and meet a silver alien
We will fly to Jupiter and we will buy some spiders
The colour of the night sky.

**Molly Sainsbury  (8)**
**Mundella Primary School**

# The Magic Box

*(Based on 'Magic Box' by Kit Wright)*

I will put in my box . . .
Three wishes that you want to come true,
A shooting star rushing through the midnight sky,
The feel of silk draped across smooth skin.

I will put in my box . . .
A slippery mountain full of snow,
The smell of crumpets cooking in the morning dew,
All the colours of the rainbow shining through clouds high above.

I will put in my box . . .
The burning sun,
A cowboy's rotten hat
And the sunniest of days.

I will put in my box . . .
The movement of the dancing flowers,
The feel of smooth petals
The sound of the drums playing,
*Bang, bang, bang.*

My box is big and covered with glittery patterns.
I will jump in the box and slide across bumpy hills.

**Jade Quigley (9)**
**Mundella Primary School**

# The Magic Box

*(Based on 'Magic Box' by Kit Wright)*

I will put in my box . . .

A pod of shining blue dolphins
The power of a unicorn's horn
Green flowery woods

I will put in my box . . .

A smell of a sandwich
A swift of sea
A smell of a Snack-a-Jack

I will put in my box . . .

A squeak of a mouse
The clap of thunder
A spark of lightning

I will put in my box . . .

The colours of the rainbow
The dark colours of the sea
The colours of a beautiful book

My box is fashioned by pink and purple spots

I will take my box to the beach and surf in the sea
After that I will bike home then I will go in the garden
And do skipping with my box.

**Saphron Packman  (9)**
**Mundella Primary School**

# The Magic Box

*(Based on 'Magic Box' by Kit Wright)*

I will put in the box . . .
A ruler that floats in the air
A white sun and a yellow moon
A soaring ten pound note

I will put in the box . . .
A triple chocolate cake with white chocolate chips
A dream of Heaven's life
A tear from the eye of truth

I will put in the box . . .
A cut from the Devil's fork
A mountain made of steel
The cage of feeling

I will put in the box . . .
A black hole leading to nowhere
The crunching of a chocolate bar
The brightest colour of green

My box is fashioned from black, silver and gold
With blue and white patterns on top
Its hinges are the bones of squirrels

I shall bury my box
On the shore of the sunny sands
Then the sand will be washed away
And it will float in the water for someone to find.

**Benjamin Gorter (9)**
**Mundella Primary School**

# The Magic Box

*(Based on 'Magic Box' by Kit Wright)*

I will put into my box . . .
A snowman that can talk to me,
A dragon that can eat you all up,
A shiny pink and red DVD player.

I will put into my box . . .
A bowl of ice cream,
A fluffy soft kitten,
A baby-pink sports car.

I will put into my box . . .
A silver and gold necklace,
A shiny ten pound note,
A silver and pink palace.

I will put into my box . . .
A bowl of strawberries that are tasty,
A white shiny and glittery smart board,
A white and baby-pink computer.

What my box looks like
A baby-blue box
And gems on the box
And it looks like a treasure box.

I am taking my box to my dad's
And me and my dad will take my box
To the place where it needs to go.

**Diamond Trice  (8)**
**Mundella Primary School**

# The Magic Box

*(Based on 'Magic Box' by Kit Wright)*

I shall put in my box . . .

The croak from a pink frog from the deep blue ocean,
The excitement and mysterious book about sea creatures,
The silk fabric from a pink and blue Superman suit.

I shall put in my box . . .

The aroma of steaming pancakes cooking,
The best rice pudding ever made,
The smell of roses growing from the ground.

I shall put in my box . . .

A little skin from the angriest crocodile,
A cup of water from the freshest sea,
The hair from the biggest bear.

My box is not fashioned but very pretty,
My box is covered with spiders, caterpillars and worms,
Which are not very tasty.

**Natalie Whitehead  (8)**
**Mundella Primary School**

# The Box Of Magic

*(Based on 'Magic Box' by Kit Wright)*

I will put into my box of magic . . .
A snowman's face with a smile made of snow
A scream of a baby at night
And the smell of a roast cooking in the oven

I will put into my box of magic . . .
A frying pan boiling hot
A rainbow of colours, all so amazing
And a swan gliding on sparkling ice

I will put into my box of magic . . .
The taste of a roast dinner bubbling in the oven
A high-pitched screaming of the wind
And the sight of gleaming stars at night

I will put into my box of magic . . .
Magic sprinkles being thrown into Heaven
The sound of church bells in a graveyard
And a heart growing bigger and bigger, full of love.

**Billie-Jo Robinson (9)**
**Mundella Primary School**

# First Dying Pet

I remember the day
Of the death of my sister's pet
I was very upset
I will never forget.

I had cried
And soaked my cover
With tears dripping non-stop from my eyes
Which tasted like bitter droplets.

After I finished crying
I went out to the back garden
It was very frosty
And the clouds were misty.

After she'd gone
I felt hollow with no one to hold and stroke
It was very upsetting
Not seeing and having her around.

**Chamange McMullen  (10)**
**Northumberland Heath Primary School**


# Loss Of A Cousin

My cousin is no longer here
In my heart I feel he is near
I miss him so much
But I can still feel his touch.

I have pictures of him
I see him as ghosts
Forever and ever
I love him most.

**William Francis  (10)**
**Northumberland Heath Primary School**

## About My Grandad!

My grandad was fab
He made me laugh
He's always in my heart
24 hours a day
He gave me sweets
But now he can't
He gave me hugs but now I feel cold.

But that day he had to go to Heaven
So he can look down on me
But I know he's OK
Because that's where he belongs
He had lots of good things about him.

But he is mine
No one can take him away from me.

**Fiona Shove  (10)**
**Northumberland Heath Primary School**

## Sadness Go Away

Sadness is black and very dark
You cry when you are sad and also sob
I hate being sad
I am scared of death and I don't want to die
I want to have health
Sadness flows like a stream that's lonely
So I say go away.

Sadness please go away
You're making my life a misery
I hate you sadness
I am telling you sadness go away
Sadness reminds me of rowing a boat.

**Philip Masheder  (9)**
**Northumberland Heath Primary School**

# When I Know Fear Is Here

When I hear crying
I think it is fear
When I hear silence
I see a tear.

When I see ghosts
I see fear
When I see devils
I know they're not here.

When I sip a drop of salt
I can taste fear
When I taste sour
I know fear is near.

When I feel empty
I feel fear
When I feel lonely
I know there's no career.

**Kimberley Webb (10)**
**Northumberland Heath Primary School**


# Boy Without A Home

I am homeless
Please help me
Get me a home
I need a home, someone
Help me find a home.

Please give me some money
For some food and drink
Please give me some money.

**Bradley Snapes (9)**
**Northumberland Heath Primary School**

# Bye-Bye My Love

I can see in the darkness
That you're all alone
But don't worry my love
You're not on your own.

I feel for you
With all my heart
I look at your picture
And I see you.

I hope you're in Heaven
Have a good time
Our son is eleven
And he thinks you're in Heaven.

Do you remember when we were one?
When we saw the sun?
Bye-bye my love forever known
Bye-bye my love you're not alone.

**Joseph Johnston (10)**
**Northumberland Heath Primary School**


# Smooth Sadness

Sadness is when you're lonely,
Maybe because the death of your pet
Because you didn't have time to take it to the vet.

I can hear screaming,
Also bells ringing,
Tears tasting like salt,
I feel it all in my throat.

**Leah Vickery-Sperinck (9)**
**Northumberland Heath Primary School**

# Happy New Start

My name is Tommie,
I am cool
And I have lots
Of friends at school.

I like ham, I like jam,
But I don't have
A computer
Or a web cam.

My sister is having a baby,
When she told me
I was running
Round like I had rabies.

All the good things
That happened in the past
I was
Always told last.

I am always
Here and I
Have no
Fear.

My heart is
Like a rocket
So that's why
It don't fit
In my pocket.

**Tommie Lee Love (10)**
**Northumberland Heath Primary School**


# Angry

When I'm angry my friends say I pull faces.
When I'm angry my mum shouts at me.
When I'm angry my sister kicks me.
When I'm angry, I'm just being me!

**Matthew Lovell (9)**
**Northumberland Heath Primary School**

# I Love My Sister

I love my sister so much,
She has a lot of luck
Because I always give her treats
And she is so nice and sweet.

She has just started in a school,
She has some friends and they're so cool.
She is at school for half a day,
She uses that time to work and play.

She is three years old
And when it's August she will be four.
When it's her birthday
She'll have presents more and more.

When I look at her
She has a great smile,
I smile back
And we play for a while.

**Sulaiman Kakay  (10)**
**Northumberland Heath Primary School**


# Care Home Kid

I am a kid in a care home
So please come and get me out.
I'll be kind,
I'll be helpful,
I'll be anything
But just please come and get me out.

It is horrible
Because bedtime is 6 o'clock,
So they say lights out.
You only get breakfast,
Nothing else,
No lunch,
So please get me out.

**Samuel Fairman  (9)**
**Northumberland Heath Primary School**

# Oh No It's Gone!

She was here yesterday
But not today,
Where has she gone?
Has she run away?

When I think of her
It reminds me of the disease.
When I look at her on my phone
I have tears in my eyes
And on a video
I'm really sad.

I will remember them
The guinea pigs they were.
This is the end of my song about my guinea pigs,
They were called Milly and Molly.

**Scott Dowsett (10)**
**Northumberland Heath Primary School**


# About My Sister

I have a sister,
I remember the first time I kissed her.
I love my sister,
Why? Why does she cry?

She lies in her cot,
She is very hot.
I get her out and comfort her in my arms,
As I rock her to sleep she starts to calm.

The happy times we have together
They will always stay with me forever.
When I gaze in her eyes she makes me smile,
I love it when she tastes my cakes.

**Jade Wilkinson (9)**
**Northumberland Heath Primary School**

## Forever Here

Oh my love you are no longer here,
I sit here alone, I sit in fear,
Oh how I miss you so much,
However I can still feel your tender touch.

I imagine in my head
You watch me till I get in my bed,
The way I sing and talk,
How I work and walk.

Our darling boys
Stopped playing with their toys,
They wonder why has gone their dad,
Asking God what has he done bad?

Oh my love you are no longer here,
I sit here alone, I sit here in fear,
Oh how I miss you so much,
However I can still feel your tender touch!

**Simran Bains (10)**
**Northumberland Heath Primary School**


## Happy

Happy is when you're having fun,
It looks like the yellow sunshine.
When I'm happy it makes me laugh.

My heart feels warm inside.
Happy is playing on the beach.
Happy is going to the park and having a good time.

**Michael Courtman (9)**
**Northumberland Heath Primary School**

# The Split Of Love

The sight of first love,
Of a wink of an eye,
But no longer more
Oh how I cry.

No longer near
But forever far,
Still I love him
He's always in my love jar.

Forever and ever I cry,
But no longer more
As I sit on the stairs
Waiting for him to come through the door.

We loved each other,
Our love was high,
I love him so
But forever I cry.

Why did we have to split?
Why do I wonder
When I think of you
It sounds like thunder.

**Kelsey McMullen  (10)**
**Northumberland Heath Primary School**


# Love

Red roses and happiness,
All I want is loveliness.
All I want is you,
I hope I never want to leave.
All I am is caring,
I will never be unkind to you.
All I need is you,
I hope we grow together.

**Tommy Bacon  (9)**
**Northumberland Heath Primary School**

# Being Angry

Have you have had that feeling
That makes you feel bad?
It's not very appealing,
Makes other people sad.

You pinch and punch,
Get all worked up,
Send people to their doom,
Your dad comes in,
Let's out a din
And sends you to your room!

Have you ever had that feeling
That makes you feel bad?
It's not very appealing,
Makes other people sad.

You shout and scream,
Your face goes red,
Be someone's death 'cause
Your mum comes in,
Let's out a din
And makes you do the chores!

**Douglas Soutar  (10)**
**Northumberland Heath Primary School**


# Love

Love is enjoyment and fun.
It feels like I'm going to my favourite place.
It feels soft and cosy and comfortable.
Love sounds like birds singing.
Love feels like when you're at home.

**Jack Holmes  (9)**
**Northumberland Heath Primary School**

# My Greatest Fear!

Snakes, snakes, snakes,
My greatest fear ever!
When I'm on holiday,
They seem to come out in the hot weather.

My heart is beating fast,
I have salty tears running down my face,
Please don't let a snake come near,
I am frightened to face my very own fear.

When I see a snake,
I feel pretty dull and cold,
But when I get over my fear,
I know I can be bold.

**Sophie Paczensky (10)**
**Northumberland Heath Primary School**


# Love

Love makes you feel sweet inside.
Love is a beautiful thing.
Love makes you feel special and warm.
Love is lovely.
Love makes you have a smile on your face.
Love is a beautiful thing.
Love is sweet.
Love is lovely.
Love gives me rosy cheeks.
Love is a beautiful thing.
Love gives me butterflies in my tummy.
Love reminds me of you.

**Skye Matczak (9)**
**Northumberland Heath Primary School**

# Sadness Of A Dream Of South Africa

Sadness, sadness that's how I'm feeling,
Cold and lonely tears taste of salt.
I've been taken from my country,
To come to England.
So now the only thing I'm relying on is going back . . .

**Ivanca Gay (9)**
Northumberland Heath Primary School


# Fear

Fear is breathtaking,
I hate fear, it's like you just want to scream.
You have fear when you have a bad dream,
But sometimes it's a dream for boys and girls.
Fear makes your heart pound,
It's like you're taking a walk off a cliff.
Fear is embarrassing but I know something
That can get rid of fear,
When you're in the dark or you're scared of heights
Just sing a song.

**Xena Djima (9)**
Northumberland Heath Primary School


# Hate

Hate is like fire burning in your stomach.
It makes you clench your teeth.
Your face goes all red.
You just want to punch them.
It ties you in a knot.

**Jake Brickwood (9)**
Northumberland Heath Primary School

# My Secret Box

*(Inspired by 'Magic Box' by Kit Wright)*

I found my box in a
Slimy, stinky sewer.

Its sides are made of lovely, warm, fluffy
Polar bear skin.

Its lid is carved from the hairy skin of a
Pompalompadomp.

Its hinges are made from a smooth,
Lovely book cover.

Inside my box I can hear the
Roaring of the Chelsea fans at Stamford Bridge.

My box feels like a
Whirlpool in the sea sucking everything that comes near.

My box inside can see the future of the world!

My box is the size of
A small football pitch/stadium.

The inside of my box smells like a
Wonka's whipple scrumptious fudge mallow delight.

My box is called a
Polarpompalmp box.

My box contains
Everything in whole wide world!

**Henry Jack Tucker  (9)**
**Palm Bay CP School**

# The Box

*(Inspired by 'Magic Box' by Kit Wright)*

I found my box
at the bottom of the garden.

Its sides are made of
stardust and moonstone.

The lid is covered from
royal purple amethyst.

The hinges are made of
the underworld's fairy dust.

Inside my box I hear the
swishing waves of the sea.

My box feels
like a bubbling spa.

Inside my box I can see
a glowing sun with a shining moon and stars.

My box is the shape of
a disguised jewellery case.

Inside my box it has the
aroma of a sweet, dainty flower.

The tips of the corners
are made of pink rose quartz.

The lid is studded with
sparkling white crystals from a fallen star.

My box contains
another dimension.

**Holly Harvey (9)**
**Palm Bay CP School**

# My Secret Box

*(Inspired by 'Magic Box' by Kit Wright)*

I found my box trapped
in Jared's long blond hair.

Its sides are made of
The spikes from a stegosaurus.

Its lid is carved out
Of a cat's fur.

Its hinges are made
Of fierce crocodile teeth.

Inside my box
I can feel the prickles of a mouse's tail.

Inside my box
I can hear the bellowing of the strictest teacher ever.

My box contains
My deep down secret.

**Bradley Welsh  (9)**
Palm Bay CP School


# My Secret Box

*(Inspired by 'Magic Box' by Kit Wright)*

I found my box
by the solid rocks.
I can see
slime with lime
with a hand,
with a motorbike's engine
and car wheels.
My box is shaped
like a UFO.
The inside smells like
a pongy cabbage field.

**Jack Brightwell  (9)**
Palm Bay CP School

# Untitled

*(Inspired by 'Magic Box' by Kit Wright)*

I found my box
caught in a spiky gooseberry bush.
Its sides are made of
glass shards from a wine goblet.
Its lid is carved from
the enamel surface of a shark's tooth.
Its hinges are made from
the spine of a grumpy gorilla.
Inside my box I can hear
the gentle waves of the beautiful sea.
My box contains
the most handsome boy in the whole universe.

**Chantelle Richardson  (9)**
**Palm Bay CP School**


# My Secret Box

*(Inspired by 'Magic Box' by Kit Wright)*

I found my box
In a mummy's body.
Its sides are made of
Willy Wonka's scrumptious chocolate.
Its lid is made of
Cursed, scaly dragon's wing.
The hinges are made from
An eyelid from an elf.
Inside my box I can see
A deserted school with a boogie monster.
My box is the shape of a UFO.
Inside my box I can hear
The roaring and screaming of Man U fans.
My box contains
A crumbling universe.

**Jordan Childs  (9)**
**Palm Bay CP School**

# My Secret Box

*(Inspired by 'Magic Box' by Kit Wright)*

I found my secret box
On the tip of a unicorn's horn.
Its sides are made of
Shark skin and dolphin teeth.
Its lid is carved from
The rough tongue of a gargoyle.
When I put any part of my body in it
I feel like the greatest king of the whole universe.
Its hinges are made from
The huge jaw of a snozwanger.
Inside my box I can hear
The mighty roar of a wangdoodle.
My box contains
All the magic you could ever imagine.
Inside my box I can see
Forty thousand of everything.
My box smells like
The boiling hot breath of a fire dragon.
My box is the shape of a T-rex head.
My box is the colour of the sparkling blue sea.
My box is secret!

**Frederick Hiscock  (9)**
Palm Bay CP School


# My Secret Box

*(Inspired by 'Magic Box' by Kit Wright)*

I found my box trapped in a bookcase.
Its sides are made from James' spiky hair
And a porcupine's quills.
Its lid is carved from the tongue of a dragon.
Its hinges are made from the jaw bones of a crocodile.
Inside my box I can hear the ocean washing against a rock.

**Olivia Brooman  (9)**
Palm Bay CP School

# My Secret Box

*(Inspired by 'Magic Box' by Kit Wright)*

I found my box
In a dark black hole.
Its sides are made from soft butterfly wings.
Its lid is made from lion's spiky fur.
Its hinges are made from Tutankhamen's golden teeth.
In my box I can hear the cheer of the giant Charlton fans.
My box's shape is a dodecahedron.
My box's colour is multicoloured.
My box smells like a beautiful red rose.
My box contains every football player in the world.

**Bradley Anderson  (8)**
**Palm Bay CP School**


# My Secret Box

*(Inspired by 'Magic Box' by Kit Wright)*

I found my box
in the bank singing opera.

Its sides are made of
earwax and blood.

Its lid is carved from
the rough skin from a lizard.

Its hinges are carved from
a ratty old letter box.

Inside my box I can hear
an eagerly desperate whale.

My box contains
the darkest, deepest secret in the world.

**Alisha Kinnon  (9)**
**Palm Bay CP School**

# My Secret Box

*(Inspired by 'Magic Box' by Kit Wright)*

I found my box
in the heart of Dr Who's Tardis.

Its sides are made of
a scaly snake's slimy skin.

Its lid is carved from
Willy Wonka's top hat.

Its hinges are made of
a shark's jaw bones.

My box feels like
a silky icy figure.

Inside my box I can see
a lovely golden statue of a paddywab.

Inside my box I can hear
a shout from a noapaz.

The inside of my box smells like
my mum's face cream.

My box contains
Rameses II price possession.

**Oliver Murphy (9)**
Palm Bay CP School


# An Unfortunate Event

Today something unfortunate happened . . .
My name is Katheryn Lamb and I like jam.
One day it was all over my face,
It looked a disgrace.

Today something unfortunate happened . . .
I tripped over a cat on a mat
And fell flat on my face
And the police were on the case.

**Katheryn Lamb (10)**
Palm Bay CP School

# My Secret Box

*(Inspired by 'Magic Box' by Kit Wright)*

I found my secret box
Break dancing in the post.
Its sides are made of
Sharks' teeth and sharks' skin.
Its lid is carved from
The teeth of a crocodile's jaw.

Its hinges are made from an
Elephant's pointy tusks.
Inside my box I can hear
The swaying sea in my ear.
Inside my box I can see
A picture of a cheeky chimpanzee.

Inside my box I can smell
A magical flower of blossom.
My box is the shape of a
White shark's fin.
My box is the colour of a
Dark, juicy red apple.

My box contains
The best secrets in the universe.

**Amy Staiger  (9)**
**Palm Bay CP School**


# City Jungle

Rusty smelly shops creep behind me.
Old damp swings hide behind children.
Old dirty cars cough loudly as they rust away.
Mouldy, creaky trees shaking as the woodpeckers peck.
Filthy damp fences crying for the owner to fix it.
Bushy black tyres groaning as they work hard.

**Kieran Somers  (9)**
**Palm Bay CP School**

# My Secret Box

*(Inspired by 'Magic Box' by Kit Wright)*

I found my fantastic box at the very bottom of the post box,
It was jammed really hard in the postbox with all the different shapes
And sizes of letters.

The sides are made of bees' wax glued together with a spider's leg.
Its lid is carved from the rough tongue of a dragon.
Its hinges are made from the jaw of a crocodile.

Inside my box I can hear
The sound of the strictest teacher in the world.

My box has got it:
A very special secret hidden in its depths.

**Chelsea Arnold (9)**
**Palm Bay CP School**


# My Secret Box

*(Inspired by 'Magic Box' by Kit Wright)*

I found my box
Hopping about in a rabbit hole.
Its sides are made from
Horses' hair.
Its lid is carved from
The horn of a unicorn.
Its hinges are made of
A robin's little claws.
Inside my box I can hear
Butterflies' soft fluttering wings.
My box smells like sweet honey.
The colour of my box is
Electric blue and lime green.
Inside my box I can see a
Huge heffalump.
My box is the shape of a
Tiny sparrow.

**Beatrice Hawkins (9)**
**Palm Bay CP School**

# My Secret Box

*(Inspired by 'Magic Box' by Kit Wright)*

I found my box in the crust of my dad's pizza.
Its sides are made of butterfly wings.
Its lid is carved out of a whale's tooth.
Its hinges are made of the jawbone of a dinosaur.
Inside my box I can hear the roar when a rhinoceros stampedes.
My box contains the stars and the moon.
My box smells like a bunch of wildflowers plucked from a sunny field.
It feels soft and looks shiny.
Inside my box I can see the rain and the sun.
My box is in the shape of a rainbow.

**Jessica Dummett  (8)**
Palm Bay CP School

# Secret Box

*(Inspired by 'Magic Box' by Kit Wright)*

I found my box
in bed sleeping.

Its sides are made of a
quilt cover.

The lid is made
with pillows.

Inside it contains
cute cuddly bears.

It is the shape of a
bed frame.

I can hear the
loud snoring of an elephant.

It is made of a
mattress.

**Elisha Kemp  (9)**
Palm Bay CP School

# An Unfortunate Event

Today something unfortunate happened,
I was riding my bike and there
Was this bird following me above
And it pooed on my head!

Today something unfortunate happened,
I was at school and I had PE
And we were doing football,
I slipped on the ball and I fell on my bum!

Today something unfortunate happened,
I had my first haircut
And I had to lean forward and when he was ready,
I leaned back and hit him in the face!

Today something unfortunate happened,
I was jumping about in my room
And it made a loud noise downstairs
And my brother pushed me into the door.

**Ashley Farbrace  (11)**
Palm Bay CP School


# An Unfortunate Event

Today something unfortunate happened,
I was on my way to school,
I fell in a humongous swimming pool,
When I got out I was dripping wet,
I got to school and asked to go home but wasn't let.

Today something unfortunate happened,
A bride was trying on her wedding dress,
It was two sizes too small,
The vicar rushed over
In his new Land Rover,
What a terrible day!

**Sophia Philpott  (10)**
Palm Bay CP School

# An Unfortunate Event

Today something unfortunate happened,
I was walking down the street,
I needed to go to the loo so I found the toilet
And by accident went in the boys.

Today something unfortunate happened,
Me, my mum and dad went swimming,
My dad dived in and his trunks fell off.

Today something unfortunate happened,
I was at school, some poor guy needed to get through
And by accident I opened my chair and hurt him.

**Jasmine Rio Hitchens  (10)**
Palm Bay CP School


# My Secret Box

*(Inspired by 'Magic Box' by Kit Wright)*

I found my box
Wedged inside a pyramid.
Its sides are made of
A branch of a thorn bush.
Its lid is heavily carved
Out of Tutankhamen's skin.
Its hinges are made of a
Kangaroo's bumpy spine.
Inside I can hear a
Duck barking at a deer.
My box contains the
Biggest secrets hidden
In the minds of English children.
Inside my box I can see
A deer eating his food and drink.
My box is the shape of
A triangular base prism.
The inside of my box
Smells like a cheesy sock.

**Chloe Griggs  (8)**
Palm Bay CP School

# An Unfortunate Event

Today something unfortunate happened,
I was riding on my bike as fast as I could
And I slipped and fell and rolled halfway down the hill into a mud pit.

Today something unfortunate happened,
I was jumping over some cars,
I jumped over one and another car came behind me and ran
me over.

Today something unfortunate happened,
I walked into the toilets and slipped
And my head fell into the toilet.

Today something unfortunate happened,
I was jumping on my trampoline
And I slipped and my tooth went into my leg.

Today something unfortunate happened,
I was in hospital and I sat on my window sill
And it smashed and I fell right to the ground.

Today something unfortunate happened,
I was running through a field of cows
And a cow chased me for three miles.

Today something unfortunate happened,
I was snowboarding on a hill,
I fell and lots of people hit me.

Today something unfortunate happened,
I was driving down a road on an icy day
And I slipped off the road and fell into a lake.

**Christopher Jordan  (10)**
**Palm Bay CP School**

# My Secret Box

*(Inspired by 'Magic Box' by Kit Wright)*

I found my box
Trapped in a CD player.

Its sides are made of
Shimmering dragon scales.

Its lid is carved from
A tiger's tooth.

Its hinge is made of
The eyelid of a killer whale.

My box feels
As cold as ice.

Inside my box I can hear
The roar of a lion.

Inside my box I can see
The future.

My box is the shape of a
Long thin cone.

Inside my box I can
Feel a burst of heat from fire.

The inside of my box smells
Like strawberries with a hint of rose.

My box contains
The answer to every question in the world.

**Charlie Sladden (9)**
**Palm Bay CP School**

# An Unfortunate Event

Today something unfortunate happened,
Today I did slip,
I had a nice trip,
I cut my knees,
No I don't want any peas.
Today something unfortunate happened,
Once I really got drunk,
I felt like a silly punk,
It was so new
I needed the loo
Because I was going to be sick
All over naughty Nick.
Today something unfortunate happened,
I love my dog
But she smells like a dirty log.
I also love my parrot,
He wants to eat a carrot.
I really have lovely pets
But they hate going to the vets.

**Jordan Morris  (10)**
Palm Bay CP School

# City Jungle

Small milk bottles swallow the milk inside them.
Big trees sneeze because of the feathers flying by.
The rotten, decayed shed coughed
When spiders crawled out of its mouth.
The postbox spits out letters as an old man puts a letter in.

**Frazer England-Fogarty  (9)**
Palm Bay CP School

# An Unfortunate Event

Today something unfortunate happened to me,
I saw a gigantic dinosaur that came to throttle me,
I picked up a green key that looked like a bottle,
It hit me on the head with a gigantic smash.

Today something unfortunate happened to me,
I took a glance at some rocks and there I stood not able to move,
Grey as a rock, grey as a lead
And there I stood with a puzzled look on my face.

Today something unfortunate happened to me,
I saw a bright pink flower,
That made me blind in the left eye.

Today something unfortunate happened to me,
I got the goosebumps
And shivered all day.

Today something unfortunate happened to me,
I saw a yellow monkey,
That swung from tree to tree.

Today something unfortunate happened to me,
I fell over in the gravel
And looked all greasy.

Today something unfortunate happened to me,
I saw a slide and wanted to go on,
But when I got on I found out it was a
Doom slide!

**Fahmina Begum  (10)**
**Palm Bay CP School**

# An Unfortunate Event

Today something unfortunate happened
Today I had a fall and fell in the mud
I hurt myself a lot and drew a bit of blood
I tried to stand up and I was a bit stuck
I pulled and pulled and pulled and I fell back in the muck.

Today something unfortunate happened
I went to the shop to buy some jeans
Instead we bought some beans
I looked a bit silly
My mum called me Billy
And I was embarrassed in the end.

Today something unfortunate happened
I went to school
And I looked like a fool
My friends slid on the ice
My mum got me some mice
I thought it was a dream
But it was true
I ended up having the flu.

**Daniel Christopher Parker  (10)**
**Palm Bay CP School**


# An Unfortunate Event

Today something unfortunate happened
Jim the fat plumber was also a drummer
Was mending a sink and fancied a drink
But he couldn't get to the cup
Because his arm was stuck!

Today something unfortunate happened
My friend Zara was riding her horse
She was calling her name and her name was Horsey
She looked away and she found herself squashed
Because she fell off.

**Lauren Katherine Grainger  (10)**
**Palm Bay CP School**

# An Unfortunate Event

Something unfortunate happened today,
My friend Zara down my road she got an electric shock.

Today something unfortunate happened,
I jumped a pool and I did not know how deep it was
And I could not swim.

Today something unfortunate happened,
My nan had a hoop and she had her shoes off
Because she was going to skip
And she fell back and it made me laugh a lot.

Today something unfortunate happened,
My cat was running up the chair
And the chair fell back and the cat was hurt.

**Sarah North  (10)**
Palm Bay CP School


# An Unfortunate Event

Today something unfortunate happened,
I was in a show,
All brave like Po,
I suddenly twitched
And looked like a witch and tripped and fell.
My mum was in the front row,
She said, 'Hello, good show,
But sad you tripped and fell.'

Today something unfortunate happened,
I was walking to school
And my mum said, 'Bye, have a cool day.'
I walked into school bursting for the loo,
And wet myself on the way,
The loo was only 5m away.

**Kayleigh Kinnon  (10)**
Palm Bay CP School

# An Unfortunate Event

Today something unfortunate happened
I was on a hill riding by bike
When suddenly it got bumpy
I tumbled over, rolled down the hill
And down into the pond.

Today something unfortunate happened
I walked into the toilet and sat down
A few minutes later I tried to stand up
But then suddenly I fell.

Today something unfortunate happened
I was cleaning the floor with a Hoover
I wasn't looking, I got stuck in
I never got out again.

Today something unfortunate happened
I was doing some stunts on my bike
When suddenly I noticed a car
It hit my tummy, it really hurt
And then I fell down dead.

Today something unfortunate happened
I was eating dinner with Mr Skinner
I came all the way from Stoke
Then started to choke on a bottle of Coke.

Today something unfortunate happened
I was on a stage doing a play
When suddenly I fell over
The crowd started to laugh, I started to cry
I felt ever so embarrassed.

**Daniel Cunningham (10)**
**Palm Bay CP School**

# Gertrude Grizzleguts

Yummy, yummy chocolate,
Yummy, yummy sweet,
In this poem there is a girl who really loved to eat!
Her name was Gertrude Grizzleguts,
She ate ten meals a day!
But still her mother fed her
And loved her come what may!
One day in Gertrude's humble home,
She pushed away a plate of food,
She said, 'Mum, I don't want it!
Not meaning to be rude!
I want something new and scrummy,
My usual grub we should lose!'
Dad sat up from the table and grabbed the Daily News,
'Well how about for yummy munch,
The Rumblitumy Island foods?'
So Gertrude set off that day,
In the hope of finding grub.
On her way a giant ate her up, munch, crunch, munch!
He spat her out in pure dismay,
She tasted like raw meat!
The moral of my poem is
Be careful what you eat!
Not meaning to sound like your mum
But eat sweets as a treat!

**Sophie Hadley (10)**
**Palm Bay CP School**

# An Unfortunate Event

Today something unfortunate happened
To the little old monk in Peru,
He dreamt he was eating a shoe.
The next morning
He was still snoring,
Then started to shout *moo! Moo!*

Today something unfortunate happened
To the old fellow Mike,
He was riding on his bike
On an enormous hike,
To find out there was a tree in front of him
And sadly he broke a limb.

Today something unfortunate happened to me,
I really, really needed a wee.
So I went to the toilet to have some privacy,
But my trousers were wet and embarrassed me.

Today something unfortunate happened
To idiot Matthew.
He ran into a wall,
A hole appeared and he started to fall.
His bottom hit the ground and he started to cry,
He really wished he could suddenly start to fly.

**Tarek Boumrah (10)**
**Palm Bay CP School**

# An Unfortunate Event

Today something unfortunate happened,
My friend gave me a scare
And I got bubblegum in my hair.
My brother said he was the king
But I had the diamond ring.

Today something unfortunate happened,
My uncle said boo
And I fell down the loo.
I fell down the stairs
And tripped over a hare.

Today something unfortunate happened,
I fell down a hole
And met a big mole.
I fell in the bin
And sat on a pin.

Today something unfortunate happened,
I fell down a wishing well
And fell on Mel.
I fell in a bush
And I went splat into the wall,
That was the end of me.

**Amba-Jo Cawte  (10)**
**Palm Bay CP School**

# An Unfortunate Event

Today something unfortunate happened to me,
I stepped into a puddle right up to the middle,
A man picked me up and sang a riddle.

Today something unfortunate happened to me,
I banged into the door,
I thought to myself *I don't need anymore!*

Today something unfortunate happened to me,
I painted my room all pink,
It looked horrible, I think!

Today something unfortunate happened to me,
I was stung by a fly,
Good, it didn't get my tie.

Today something unfortunate happened to me,
I fell into a rubbish bin,
Cor! I just couldn't win!

Today something unfortunate happened to me,
I tried to run a race,
I fell over and hurt my face!

Today something unfortunate happened to me,
I saw an apple tree,
I banged into it. It hurt me!

Today some things just didn't go right,
Got to go now, goodnight!

**Rosie Raven  (10)**
**Palm Bay CP School**

# An Unfortunate Event

Today something unfortunate happened,
A man was doing some car stunts,
He drove and flipped over some large trucks.
He zoomed into the air
Without one single care
And landed with a large thump.
He got out of the car
And said, 'Tada!'
And a big lorry ran him over!

Today something unfortunate happened,
There was a lady
Who had a baby
And went a bit crazy,
She went to the beach
And decided to preach.
She thought the sea was glass
And decided to swim,
That poor old lady
And that baby,
Now they're nothing but a memory.

Today something unfortunate happened,
A lady went to the shop by a drain,
She bought something that came from Spain.
She got out her purse
And then said a curse,
Because she dropped her money down the drain.

**Phoebe Allen  (10)**
**Palm Bay CP School**

# An Unfortunate Event

Today something unfortunate happened,
I fell in a well
And thought I was going to Hell.
I fell in some water,
It smelt like slaughter,
I couldn't get out again.
Today something unfortunate happened,
I went to a shop
To buy some fizzy pop,
I got out my purse,
I found on it a curse,
I was very scared indeed.
Today something unfortunate happened,
I put on my frock,
I put my hair in curly locks,
I found myself covered in warts and spots,
I can't go out like that!
Today something unfortunate happened,
I went for a walk,
I had a little chat,
I went back home
And found on the phone
An unusual little clone.
Today something unfortunate happened,
I went to school,
I fell in a pool,
It didn't look cool.
I made myself a complete utter fool,
I won't go to school again.

**Jessie-Jo Epps  (10)**
**Palm Bay CP School**

# An Unfortunate Event

Today something unfortunate happened,
I fell in the mud,
Looked up to find a smelly pug,
It looked ill,
Like it had a bill,
But still it tried to kill me.

Today something unfortunate happened,
I tripped on the path,
No one laughed
Except for one girl on the path,
Nevertheless I looked down
To find I had landed in dog mess.

Today something unfortunate happened,
I lay on hay in May,
I'd fallen off a ladder into a clatter of cans,
All the old nans came over with pans
And whacked the evil man-killer lambs.

**Holly Rebecca Austen  (10)**
Palm Bay CP School


# City Jungle

Loud revving sports cars run by to get out of the rain.
Gurgling drains swallow gallons of pouring rainwater.
Towering houses sneeze in the freezing cold wind.
Hungry garages chew up fast entering cars.
Rotten, decayed sheds begging to be restored.
Big black street lamps blink on as the sky darkens.
Filthy blue wheelie bins wheel around.

**Aaron Barnett  (9)**
Palm Bay CP School

# City Jungle

Dingy, rusty dustbins swallow disgusting rubbish enthusiastically.
Nasty, smelly houses creep behind you with their shoulders hunched.
Boisterous leaves scurry energetically past you trying to find
the gutter.
Fragile milk bottles shiver at dusk.
Rusty dirt covered swings sit all alone.
Old rotting bags scurry to cover.

**James Mulligan  (10)**
Palm Bay CP School

# City Jungle

Rotten cans scurry away from dirty dingy dustbins
And creep under cars.
Postboxes sneeze out letters and sniffle them back in.
Dirty, dingy dustbins drink the falling rain from the heavenly skies.
Filthy plastic bags scamper across the black tarry road.
Rotten and dingy dustbins, decayed sheds spit out spiders from
years ago.
Burnished gleaming benches wink at their garden friends.

**Thomas Syson-Warwick  (9)**
Palm Bay CP School

# City Jungle

Dingy, rusty dustbins swallow rubbish lazily.
Shiny red postbox chewing, slopping all the letters.
Nasty, creepy houses sneakily flowing behind you.
Rusty, rattly dustbins swallowing dirty rubbish.
White shiny milk bottles cleaning, sipping milk.
Shiny lamp posts swaying their gumming rusty teeth.
Dark scary drainpipes bumping roughly at the rustling wind.
Noisy, rumbling vehicles rambling through the cool wind.

**Deanna Basson**
Palm Bay CP School

# City Jungle

Rusty, dingy dustbins swallow up rotten rubbish in the cold
breezy wind.
Drains hide at the side of the road as they chew up the
freezing water.
Shops hunch in the cold wind, as soft snow lands gently on their roofs.
Posh new convertibles smile proudly as they screech round corners.
Rotten, decayed sheds cry out to be restored as a piece of wood
flakes off.
Drenched, durable drain pipes regurgitate stagnant water.

**George Walton (9)**
Palm Bay CP School


# City Jungle

Damp, rotting leaves scurry across the moist concrete.
Bright, burnished headlights blink through the misty night.
Dingy, rusty dustbins swallow the freezing cold rainwater as it
howls past.
Wet old bushes hide behind hunched-up houses shivering in
the wind.
Tall slender street lamps stare at the tarmacy ground.
Filthy, rustling plastic bags jump across the wet pavement as
the wind sneaks past.
Black rusty gutters gulp down gallons of stagnant cold water.

**Amy Holland (9)**
Palm Bay CP School


# City Jungle

Moss covered gutters swallow the rainwater as it dribbles in.
Tall skyscraper trees hunch together as the woodpeckers come past.
The ghostly headlights stare into the open air.
The lamp post blinks as the storm hits its delicate head.
The benches cough as people jump on it.
The leaf-collecting shed gives a little cry as people walk past.

**Jake Vial (9)**
Palm Bay CP School

# City Jungle

Moist, old damp trees hunch together as the blowing wind howls by.
Gutters rusty and dingy lay on the ground drinking all the rain
as it flows into its mouth.
Plastic bags filthy and rustling jumping frantically from street to street.
Sheds, all rotten and chipped moaning and coughing
as another spider crawls on his windpipe.

**Paul Baker (9)**
Palm Bay CP School

# City Jungle

Moist, moss-covered drains burp out bubbles of gas into the
midnight sky.
Ice-cool, lustrous blue convertibles laugh proudly as they zoom
past people.
Glamorous, blood-red postboxes slouch tiredly whilst waiting
to be reused.
A rotting, decaying shed crying out to be restored.
Filthy, ripped plastic carrier bags leap around happily now that
they've got freedom.
Multicoloured traffic lights wink teasingly at cars as they drive by.

**Cameron Roan Hardwick (9)**
Palm Bay CP School

# City Jungle

Rusty, greasy, black gutters lay creepily in the middle of the ground.
Huge, bright, colourful swings laugh as little children play happily
on them.
Rusty old gates creak open and sit gloomily by themselves.
Rotten, decayed wooden sheds sit gloomily by themselves choking
on spiders.
A filthy, rustling plastic bag shuffles around the black streets
shivering because of the coldness.

**Kate Warburton (10)**
Palm Bay CP School

# City Jungle

The swings sway happily in the fast blowing wind.
The moss-covered wall slouches in the skin-chilling snow.
The unexamined leaves scurry into the air soaring through the sky.
The arrogant cars brag about how good their modified sports
                                                    engines are.
The whimpering shed, as decaying as ever, coughs grumpily in
                                                    the morning cold.
The dangerous looking motorbikes blink savagely at the
                                                    durable road.

**Darrioush Zahedi (10)**
Palm Bay CP School


# City Jungle

The lamp post covered in rust and disgusting screams
Because the builder is cutting it down.
Cars run by the lamp post and always make it even more scared.
Long tall trees burp and cry.
Trees always drink and sneeze.
Plastic bags always fight when the cars zoom by.
Postbox always moans when the paper flies away.

**Oli Rahman (9)**
Palm Bay CP School


# An Unfortunate Event

Today something unfortunate happened to me,
I walked without my socks on
And stepped on a bee,
I hoped it wouldn't sting me.

Today something unfortunate happened to me,
I went to cubs, I got a paper cut,
Then I went to golf
And couldn't even putt.

**John Christopher Forster (10)**
Palm Bay CP School

# City Jungle

Red-eyed cars leap round the vast road.
Huge trees reach up into the sky like a skeleton's bones
Reaching up to the pale moon.
The large postbox coloured as red as blood
Gurgles at cars passing by.
Massive buildings and lamp posts snigger down from their
vantage point.
Skyscrapers wave at passing pedestrians who bother to look at them.
Smelly corroded dustbins swallow up the circling leaves.
The splintered gates look like someone with a bad hair day.
Garages groan as they are viciously opened.

**Edward Martin (9)**
Palm Bay CP School

# City Jungle

Tall thin trees whisper quietly in the nippy cold air.
Moss-covered gutters gurgle down filthy rainwater filling them
to the top.
Small damp leaves scuttle along the roadside forced to move
by the wind.
Bright red postboxes hold all your letters protecting them from
the rain.
Rain-filled clouds float across the glistening sky hiding behind
the moonlight.
Happy pink pansies wave hello to the vast bushes behind them
in your back garden.

**Megan Liddell (9)**
Palm Bay CP School

# An Unfortunate Event

Today something unfortunate happened to my brother,
He was jumping in lots of mud
And he saw that there was a small lump of mud
And jumped in it but it wasn't mud it was dogs' droppings.

Today something unfortunate happened to my friend,
He was leaning back on his chair
And the next thing you know he ended up on the ground
And said, 'Ouch,' in a silent hard sound.

Today something unfortunate happened to me,
I was in a lift going to my dad's flat to see him
And all of a sudden the lift broke down
And I shouted, 'Help, help!' and then I soon got out.

**Emma Saunders  (10)**
**Palm Bay CP School**

# City Jungle

Towering street lamps yawn
and finally fall asleep,
leaving the street dark and dejected.

Rusty dustbins heave with
the weight of decaying Chinese
containers and leftover roast.

Abandoned and alone crisp packets
and beer cans are left
to wander the streets in dismay.

A plastic bag disturbs the
gravel as it's dragged underneath
the wheels of an oncoming car.

Frantic swings scream
and give way to the howling wind
for they have no fight left
within their chains and more
importantly their hearts.

**Katie Baldock  (9)**
**Palm Bay CP School**

# City Jungle

Long, gargantuan lorries rumble over the bumpy road.
A stinky, horrible odour rides the gusts of wind.
A famished, lustrous dustbin gobbles up a bag of scented rubbish.
Classy, sports cars' engines cough out dense black smoke.
A modest, parched postbox shivers as rats scurry past.
Brown, blemished leaves leap in the freezing cold air.
A vulnerable, shivering ring cries as its owner walks out into the
misty, foggy night.
A rotten, decayed shed yawns open its creaky door.
Drenched drainpipes regurgitate out the stagnant water into
the sewage.
Tall, polished lights stare out their lustrous colours.

**Rory Middleton  (10)**
Palm Bay CP School


# City Jungle

The mouldy rotten trees sway under the weight of the water in
their roots.
The crushed cans run erratically along the road.
The rusty old lamp post leans over in the wind.
The smelly, reeking dustbins gulp in tons of rubbish.
The blood-red postbox burps out letters.
The night-black limousine speeds along the black tarmac of the
world proudly.
The broken fences moan in the air, while the flakes of groaning
gates come off.

**Pablo Garcia Thomas  (9)**
Palm Bay CP School

# City Jungle

Shiny damp cans scurry along in the wind.
The blood-red postbox burps out dripping rainwater.
Transparent, wet milk bottles gargle the leftover milk.
Hunched brown houses huddle up together.
Deserted, creaking swings cling together.
Glamorous, metallic lamp posts bare their brilliant white teeth.
Tall, slender drain pipes grip onto the houses.
Filthy, rustling plastic bags jump along in the morning wind.
Shiny white people carriers trudge down my street.

**Grace Ellisdon (10)**
Palm Bay CP School


# City Jungle

Dustbins rusty, smelly, rotten chew up rubbish that has been discarded
into them.
Gates chipped, rough, splinter-covered hide behind a tree when
they know someone is coming.
Trees mysterious and quiet creep round the woods so the
woodpeckers will not chip them.
Plastic bags dirty and ripped jump across the street as the
gusty wind pushes them.
Gutters moss-covered and damp lay quietly on the ground not making
a sound, afraid to be seen.
Cans, rusty, dirty cans choking up flies as they fly into it trying
to make a home.

**Charlotte Tonkiss (9)**
Palm Bay CP School

# My Cats

We have four cats in my house,
They're as different as chalk and cheese,
Each has their own personality
And generally do as they please.

Smudge, now he's the biggest,
Mostly white, a real cool dude,
He roams the streets and gets filthy,
He's a cat with attitude.

Bella, she's the smallest,
Brown and furry with a fluffy type mane,
But she's always first at feeding times,
She's a queen in her domain.

George, now he's the loudest,
Black and white, but a real scaredy cat,
He's so quick when catching mice outside,
But at loud noises, this cat scats.

Holly, now she's the quiet one,
You hardly know she's there,
She's as silent as a shadow,
Till she legs it up the stairs.

**James Hannah (11)**
**St Eanswythe's CE (A) Primary School, Folkestone**

# Love

I love my mum
And I love my dad
And I love my sister
And I love my brother
And I love my cat
And I love my nanny
And I love my grandad.

**Brittany Cousins (7)**
**St Eanswythe's CE (A) Primary School, Folkestone**

# Flowers

F lowers are pretty,
L ovely they are,
O h, I have so many, they are
W onderful, lovely, some are
E normous, some are tiny,
R un through meadows of flowers,
S ome flowers are pretty, others

A re not, anyway,
R unning through a meadow just
E mpty your mind and imagine

P retty flowers, just let it
R un through your
E ducated mind, let it run
T hrough, just let it run
T hrough, run through
Y our mind.

**Aimée Thomson  (8)**
**St Eanswythe's CE (A) Primary School, Folkestone**


# The Mongrel

The mongrel is a specific dog,
He leaps, he jumps and chews a log,
But, as he drinks from the bog,
He thinks to himself,
I have the paw of a pointer
And the body of a dingo,
What breed should I be?
Because, I never see a dog that looks like me,
But all I know now is that I'm a dog,
And I will always be one.

**Trevyn Rayner-Canham  (9)**
**St Eanswythe's CE (A) Primary School, Folkestone**

# The Firelight Night

This way and that
In the firelight night
Forward and back
In the firelight night
Up and down
In the firelight night
All around
In the firelight night

The stars are bright
In the firelight night
The moon white
In the firelight night
The dew twinkling
In the firelight night
The chimes tinkling
In the firelight night
Falling asleep
In the firelight night.

**Jordan Neagle  (11)**
**St Eanswythe's CE (A) Primary School, Folkestone**


# Dog In The Frame

A trainer chewer
A homework stealer
A toilet dropper
A water gulper
A mad eater
A fast sprinter
A loud barker
A cute face.

**Paige Baigent  (11)**
**St Eanswythe's CE (A) Primary School, Folkestone**

# My Secret Garden

In my dreams there is a place,
Where warm wind blows and warms your face.

The sun shines brightly in the sky,
Singing bluebirds pass me by.
Sweet smell of roses all around,
Grass of green upon the ground.

Busy bees and butterflies in the summer air,
Rabbits, cats and puppy dogs playing everywhere.

Underneath the old oak tree the fairies are asleep,
Mustn't make a single noise, shh, not a little peep.

In the stream upon a log,
There sits grumpy Mr Frog.
In the flowers, coloured pink,
There lives a skunk, called Mr Stink.

Every night when daytime ends,
I go to sleep and see my friends.

Goodbye my secret garden, now the day has come,
I'll see you in my dreams again, when the day is done.

**Kimberly Stephens  (8)**
**St Eanswythe's CE (A) Primary School, Folkestone**


# Flowers

Roses are red like the red in a rainbow.
Violets are blue like the blue in the sky.
Blossom is pink like the pink on my pen.
Daffodils are yellow like the yellow in the sun.
Snowdrops are white like the white crisp snow
And the stems of the flowers are as green as the grass.
All of these things you find in a garden,
Forever to look at and never to pass.

**Charlotte Edgar  (9)**
**St Eanswythe's CE (A) Primary School, Folkestone**

# The Mermaid

She lives in Merworld under the sea,
A thousand miles down as far as can be.
She swims to the surface and loves to view
The humans on land, that's me and you.
She swims to the bottom very fast
And finds an old music box straight from the past.
She swims to the palace, what a wonderful sight,
Beautiful music and dancing fills her with delight.
Her bath is a shell,
Her comb is an old fork,
She plays catch with a pearl
And she sings when she talks.
Her world is a beautiful place to be,
That wonderful Merworld under the sea.

**Francesca Marsh (9)**
St Eanswythe's CE (A) Primary School, Folkestone


# My Troll

The troll that lives beneath my bed
Has purple dreadlocks on his head
And orange skin and yellow eyes,
It looks like custard if he cries.

I go to bed and watch TV,
He jumps around and tickles me.
He flicks my dog and hides my mouse,
He causes chaos in our house.

Today he stole my purple vest,
That troll I say is such a pest.
The things he does no one can see,
So everybody thinks it's me.

**Tula Williamson (8)**
St Eanswythe's CE (A) Primary School, Folkestone

# My Nan And Grandad

While Grandad's sleeping in his chair
I tied pink ribbons in his hair.
My nan she laughs and thinks it's funny
And gives me extra pocket money.

Nan's pink lipstick for the finishing touch,
I've never seen my nan laugh so much.
When Grandad wakes he feels his hair
And says, 'Come on, this isn't fair.'

He gives the ribbons a little tug,
Grabs me quick and gives me a hug.
Time to go home back to my mum
And tell her all about our fun.

They are always happy and never show sorrow,
Goodbye Grandad, I'll be back tomorrow.

**Hayley Brickell (11)**
**St Eanswythe's CE (A) Primary School, Folkestone**


# Santa And Snow

Winter's day in the garden,
When Jack Frost never says pardon,
Up and down, round and round the snowflakes jump,
Even in the flowerpot.

Santa is here on the roof,
I tell you right I have some proof.
Santa's hat all red and furry with a ball on top,
You can hear the reindeer hooves going clip-clop.
So sleep now my dear
Because Christmas is near.

**Sophie Thomson (10)**
**St Eanswythe's CE (A) Primary School, Folkestone**

# Snow

Snow is falling, snow is falling
Out of the sky.
Sleet is falling, sleet is falling
From very high.

You can make a snowman,
Or have a fight,
Let's hope it snows all night.

We can skid on the ice
And sledge down the hills
And take a family hike in the fields,
But make sure you wear gloves, hats and scarves
'Cause it's very cold and the snow will cover the paths.

Snow is melting, snow is melting,
The sun is coming out,
Winter is nearly over and that's a fact
Without a doubt.

**Bethany Read (10)**
**St Eanswythe's CE (A) Primary School, Folkestone**


# Christmas Comes

Christmas time when reindeer run,
Christmas time when Santa comes.
Christmas time when it snows,
Christmas time when it glows.
Christmas time when you sleep,
Christmas time when you sneak.
Christmas time is a special time,
Remember Christmas time.

**Connor Green (8)**
**St Eanswythe's CE (A) Primary School, Folkestone**

# Sunlight Ruined

*Swish, swoosh* . . .
The calm sea feathering the sand,
Mint-fresh air, yum!
Fluffy cotton wool clouds making way for the sun
But that's just an image of someone's wish,
Really it's just a dramatic storm gale of 75mph.
*Gush, gush* the sea roars raging with anger,
*Weep, weep* the clouds are crying . . .
The sun is lost.

**Mariam Quraishi  (11)**
**St Eanswythe's CE (A) Primary School, Folkestone**


# A Football Poem

I'm a leg breakin', goal scorin'
Referee fightin', net breakin'
Crowd booin', supporter fightin'
England losin', Portugal winnin'
Crouch crouchin', defenders leapin'
Players cryin', crowd cheerin'
Shirt pullin', Crouch trippin'
Cool scorin', match winnin'
Celebratin' *midfielder!*

**Rémy Cabache  (10)**
**St Eanswythe's CE (A) Primary School, Folkestone**


# Winston - Cinquain

My dog
Is called Winston
He sleeps a lot, snoring
In my bedroom, he is asleep
Winston.

**Alice Copeland  (9)**
**St Katharine's Knockholt CE (A) Primary School, Knockholt**

# Lunch Box

One day I got taken to school
And when I got there I sat in the hall.
I waited and waited
And absolutely hated
Waiting all day in the hall.

Finally I got taken to lunch
For my owner to munch and munch.
He ate and ate
With his mate,
Oh how I like being taken to lunch.

**Emily Hinchcliffe  (10)**
St Katharine's Knockholt CE (A) Primary School, Knockholt


# Snow Dream

Darkness then light
Eyes awaken from
Nervous night.

Rough carpet
Under feet
Window blinds
Hide falling sleet.

Crunching snow
Now lies deep
Down the path
My wellies creep.

Down the road
An old man walks
To anyone else
He never talks.

**Charlie McKechnie  (9)**
St Katharine's Knockholt CE (A) Primary School, Knockholt

# A Friend

As we met in the playground,
A friendship was soon found,
She is a great parade of fun,
My friend Kirsty.

The face like a lullaby,
That makes me want to fly,
Orange hair like autumn leaves,
My friend Kirsty.

A piece of string that will not end,
The best of a good friend,
Brown eyes like melted chocolate,
My friend Kirsty.

Kirsty's flame will not go out,
We're best mates without a doubt,
Her face is a song of greatness,
My friend Kirsty.

**Amy Callaghan  (10)**
**St Katharine's Knockholt CE (A) Primary School, Knockholt**


# My Dogs - Cinquains

My Ted
Rottweiler dog
Big, strong, muscly boy
When I open the door he jumps
On me.

My Flo
A small fast dog
She sits, begs, rolls over
When I go to bed she snuggles
With me.

**Joe Copeland  (10)**
**St Katharine's Knockholt CE (A) Primary School, Knockholt**

# Snow

Falling down, swirling around
And settles on the ground.
Children shouting and screaming,
It is on the ground white and gleaming.
The snow is bright like the sun,
Everybody is having fun.
On the road it is very wet,
But on the field the snow has set.

**Ruby Cooper (10)**
St Katharine's Knockholt CE (A) Primary School, Knockholt

# The Old Brown Horse - Cinquain

Old horse
Shakes his old head
Wearily runs to gate
So lonely he stands by himself
Old horse.

**Emily Smith (10)**
St Katharine's Knockholt CE (A) Primary School, Knockholt

# Football - Cinquain

Football
Marching on pitch
Playing to victory
All day long scoring goals in net
Football.

**Joshua John Walker (9)**
St Katharine's Knockholt CE (A) Primary School, Knockholt

# My Dog - Cinquains

My dog
Her name's Scooby
Short fur, brown flapping ears
Wagging tail, brown eyes watching me
Sweet face.

Running
Around with her
Playing fetch on the grass
Sitting on the floor stroking her
Love her.

**Kirsty Tapsell  (10)**
**St Katharine's Knockholt CE (A) Primary School, Knockholt**

# Fishing - Cinquain

Sitting
And waiting for
A fish to take interest
In my delicious squirming worm
Yum-yum!

**Ben Charman  (10)**
**St Katharine's Knockholt CE (A) Primary School, Knockholt**

# Football Team - Cinquain

Football
Which team to choose
Liverpool, Arsenal
Reading, Charlton and Tottenham
I like . . .

**Cameron Essam  (11)**
**St Katharine's Knockholt CE (A) Primary School, Knockholt**

# School - Cinquains

School time,
Maths, maths, maths time,
Boring teacher droning
On and on and on and on and . . .
No more!

Home time,
No more teacher,
No more school and droning,
Hooray, hooray, hooray, hooray,
Hometime!

**Keturah Paice  (9)**
St Katharine's Knockholt CE (A) Primary School, Knockholt

# Doogie - Cinquain

My boy,
Fluffy and white,
My little boy, Westie,
Lots of nicknames for him to choose
Doogie.

**Daisy Bell  (10)**
St Katharine's Knockholt CE (A) Primary School, Knockholt

# Spitfire - Cinquain

Spitfire,
Shoot enemy,
Fire, fire, fire, hit, hit, hit,
Messerschmitt at twelve o'clock, fire,
Success.

**Peter Roper  (10)**
St Katharine's Knockholt CE (A) Primary School, Knockholt

# Ice-Skating - Cinquains

Arrive
At the ice rink
Hand in your boots and get
Ice skates back, stepping on the ice
Splat, ow.

Get up
Grab the side, push
Gliding across the ice
Wobble, I think I am going
To fall.

**Jessica Hudson  (10)**
**St Katharine's Knockholt CE (A) Primary School, Knockholt**


# Hamsters - Cinquain

Hamsters
Hamsters are sweet
I have three dwarf hamsters
They can run very, very fast
Hamsters.

**Tilly Johnson  (10)**
**St Katharine's Knockholt CE (A) Primary School, Knockholt**


# Mars Bars - Cinquain

Mars bars
Very yummy
I love them lots and lots
I think Mars bars are really great
Yum-yum.

**Indianna Bareham  (10)**
**St Katharine's Knockholt CE (A) Primary School, Knockholt**

# My Pet - Cinquain

My pet
Is called Tigger
He prefers dried cat food
He likes to sit on wooden chairs
Tigger.

**William McLoughlin  (10)**
St Katharine's Knockholt CE (A) Primary School, Knockholt


# Football - Cinquain

Football
Stadium loud
Steven Gerrard scores goal
Crowds go ecstatically crazy
Winners.

**Alexander Rogers  (10)**
St Katharine's Knockholt CE (A) Primary School, Knockholt


# Snow

S  lippery snow is on the ground
N  aughty children are getting sent in
O  verthrown snowballs hitting the teachers
W  hen will this chaos end?

**George Harber  (10)**
St Katharine's Knockholt CE (A) Primary School, Knockholt


# River - Haiku

Rushing and gushing
And flowing quite rapidly
Towards the ocean.

**Ben McKechnie  (11)**
St Katharine's Knockholt CE (A) Primary School, Knockholt

# Snow

Very nervous
As I pull back the curtain,
Excited at the sight of
Deep, deep snow.

The crunch of snow
Under wellies,
Cold numb toes,
Footprints reveal paths.

Snow flying
Like crystal shining,
Little boy crying
With a white face.

Sun is shining,
White is disappearing,
All alone
In the melted snow.

**Jak Colley  (9)**
**St Katharine's Knockholt CE (A) Primary School, Knockholt**


# Swimming - Cinquain

Diving
Freezing water
Racing against your friends
Hit the slide, tumble turn, gliding
Surface.

**Olivia Harbard  (10)**
**St Katharine's Knockholt CE (A) Primary School, Knockholt**

# A Snowy Day

Brightness all around
Cold air
Frozen, chilly snow
Like a white blanket.

Icy roads
Sparkling, shining snow
The pale diamonds glistening
Winter has come.

The fresh smell of freezing snow
Falling all around
The coldness of that shivery snowy day
Snowflakes as white as white.

The children playing with snowballs
Deeper their boots sink
In the snow
Their scarves all purple and pink.

**Emma Pound  (9)**
**St Katharine's Knockholt CE (A) Primary School, Knockholt**


# Snowball Fight

A ball made
of snow flying
through the air,
about to hit someone,
they dodged and
dived onto the ground
with a crunch.
I built another one quick,
I threw it
and hit him.

**Sam Link  (10)**
**St Katharine's Knockholt CE (A) Primary School, Knockholt**

# Snow

A gleam of whiteness
Comes through my windows;
A white winter wonderland
Waits for me outside.

One step in the untouched snow.
With a crunch and a crackle,
It freezes my toes;
They feel numb inside my wellies.

My nose starts to run
As I take another step.
I step right into the tingling fun,
While there's snow on the trees' branches.

Animal footprints everywhere,
As I start to make snowmen.
In the cold, cold air
I like snow very, very much.

**Emma-Louise Richardson (10)**
**St Katharine's Knockholt CE (A) Primary School, Knockholt**


# My Mum

My mum,
She loves and cares,
Would do anything to hold me tight in her arms,
She cares about me.

My mum,
I would do so much to cuddle with her,
Would never end,
I would do anything for her.

**James Robins (10)**
**St Katharine's Knockholt CE (A) Primary School, Knockholt**

# My Mum's Day Out

My mum is having a day out
So she's got some animals helping us out with the chores,

There's a . . .
Grumpy gorilla gardening,
A wet wallaby washing,
A colourful cheetah cooking,
A posh poodle painting,
A hairy horse hoovering,
A painful piranha punishing,
An intelligent iguana ironing,
A slithering snake shopping,
A flaming frog frying,
A pretty parrot polishing.

We now have a very clean house,
Thanks to the animals that helped us out.

**Sarah Pickering (10)**
St Katharine's Knockholt CE (A) Primary School, Knockholt

# Spencer - Cinquains

Spencer
Has a big coat
Long golden fluffy fur
He is a golden retriever
Our dog.

Spencer
Is a big dog
He can catch a fast ball
He jumps up at me and licks me
Yuck, yuck.

**Daniel Waldron (11)**
St Katharine's Knockholt CE (A) Primary School, Knockholt

# Young Writers Information

We hope you have enjoyed reading this book - and that you will continue to enjoy it in the coming years.

If you like reading and writing poetry drop us a line, or give us a call, and we'll send you a free information pack.

Alternatively if you would like to order further copies of this book or any of our other titles, then please give us a call or log onto our website at www.youngwriters.co.uk

**Young Writers Information
Remus House
Coltsfoot Drive
Peterborough
PE2 9JX**

**(01733) 890066**